# CONTENTS

GRADE 4

## UNIT 1 SENTENCES

**GRAMMAR** SENTENCES

**BUILD SKILLS**

McGraw-Hill School Division

# UNIT 2 NOUNS

## GRAMMAR  NOUNS

## BUILD SKILLS

# UNIT 3 VERBS

● **GRAMMAR** VERBS

## BUILD SKILLS

McGraw-Hill School Division

# UNIT 4 ADJECTIVES

**GRAMMAR** ADJECTIVES

## BUILD SKILLS

# UNIT 5 PRONOUNS

**GRAMMAR** PRONOUNS

**BUILD SKILLS**

McGraw-Hill School Division

# UNIT 6   ADVERBS AND PREPOSITIONS

McGraw-Hill School Division

# Sentences

---
**┌ RULES ═══════════════════════════════════════════**

- A **sentence** is a group of words that expresses a complete thought. A sentence names the person or thing you are talking about. It also tells what happened.

  SENTENCE: *I received a letter from my pen pal.*

- A **sentence fragment** is a group of words that does not express a complete thought.

  FRAGMENT: *Friends for a long time.*

---

Read each group of words. Circle **yes** if the words make a sentence. Circle **no** if they are a sentence fragment.

| | | |
|---|---|---|
| 1. Maritza is my favorite pen pal. | **yes** | **no** |
| 2. Lives in Puerto Rico. | **yes** | **no** |
| 3. I have been writing to Maritza for two years. | **yes** | **no** |
| 4. She is four months older than me. | **yes** | **no** |
| 5. Tall girl with green eyes. | **yes** | **no** |
| 6. We are both in the fourth grade. | **yes** | **no** |
| 7. I visited Puerto Rico with my family. | **yes** | **no** |
| 8. Stayed at Maritza's house. | **yes** | **no** |
| 9. Maritza introduced me to all her friends. | **yes** | **no** |
| 10. Sometimes her brother. | **yes** | **no** |

McGraw-Hill School Division

10 **McGraw-Hill Language Arts
Grade 4, Unit 1, Sentences,
pages 2–3**

**At Home:** Choose a sentence fragment from this page. Add words to make it a sentence. Write your new sentence on a separate sheet of paper.

1

# Declarative and Interrogative Sentences

┌─ **RULES** ─────────────────────────────────────────────┐

• A **declarative sentence** makes a statement.

       *My pen pal lives in Japan.*

It begins with a **capital letter.**      It ends with a **period.**

• An **interrogative sentence** asks a question.

       *Where does your pen pal live?*

It begins with a **capital letter.**      It ends with a **question mark.**

└──────────────────────────────────────────────────────────┘

Draw one line under each sentence that makes a statement. Draw two lines under each sentence that asks a question.

1. My funny letter is in my pocket.

2. Do you need to buy stamps?

3. I will mail my letter at the post office.

4. Many customers are waiting in line.

5. There are three women and two men behind me.

6. How many packages will be mailed today?

7. What is in the big envelope?

8. It contains postcards from Japan.

9. Sayuri, my pen pal, sends me wonderful presents.

10. Can you think of something she would like from the United States?

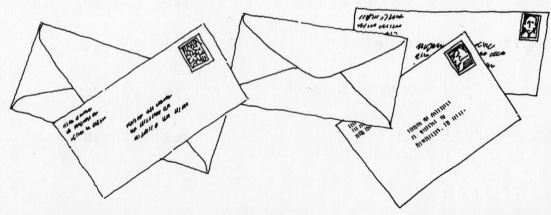

**At Home:** Write two sentences about the state you live in. Then write two questions that you would ask Sayuri about Japan.

**McGraw-Hill Language Arts Grade 4, Unit 1, Sentences, pages 4–5**

2

/10

McGraw-Hill School Division

# Imperative and Exclamatory Sentences

┌─ **RULES** ─────────────────────────────────────────────────┐

• An **imperative sentence** tells or asks someone to do something.

*Cook the rice and beans for twenty minutes.*

It begins with a **capital letter.**      It ends with a **period.**

• An exclamatory sentence shows strong feeling.

*What a delicious dinner you prepared!*

It begins with a **capital letter.**      It ends with an **exclamation mark.**

└─────────────────────────────────────────────────────────────┘

Draw one line under each sentence that tells or asks someone to do something. Draw two lines under each sentence that shows strong feeling.

1. Please help set the table.

2. It's surprising how many are coming!

3. Put the flowers on the table.

4. What a mess I made!

5. Don't forget to take out the garbage.

6. Watch for our guests, please.

7. How tired I am!

8. Turn on the radio and close the window.

9. Oh no, I broke a glass!

10. Wow, this is a big party!

McGraw-Hill School Division

10

**McGraw-Hill Language Arts**
Grade 4, Unit 1, Sentences,
pages 6–7

**At Home:** Draw a funny picture. Write three exclamatory sentences to go with your picture.

3

# Combining Sentences: Compound Sentences

┌─ **RULES** ─────────────────────────────────────

- A compound sentence is made up of two sentences joined by *and, or,* or *but.*

- Use a comma (,) before *and, or,* or *but* when you write a compound sentence.

   *This is a zoo, **but** animals are not in cages.*

   *We can visit the new zoo, **or** we can go to the planetarium.*

   *Some keepers feed the zoo animals, **and** other people study the animals.*

┌─────────────────────────
│ **Conjunction Box**
│
│ **and** - links ideas
│ **but** - shows contrast
│ **or** - shows choice
└─────────────────────────

Underline the conjunction in each compound sentence. Then write it on the line.

1. Natasha and I watched the monkeys, but we didn't feed them.                    _____

2. Zookeepers know what kind of food each animal eats, and they know how much it needs.          _____

3. Wild animals can get their own food, but zoo animals must be fed by keepers.              _____

4. Lions don't eat every day in the wild, and they're not fed every day in the zoo, either.         _____

5. Next month we will visit a museum, or we will go back to the zoo.                  _____

McGraw-Hill School Division

## Mechanics and Usage: Sentence Punctuation

> **RULES**
>
> Every sentence begins with a capital letter.
>
> • A **declarative sentence** makes a statement.
>   It ends with a **period.** *The contest begins Friday night.*
>
> • An **interrogative sentence** asks a question.
>   It ends with a **question mark.** *Who will be the winner?*
>
> • An **imperative sentence** tells or asks someone to do something.
>   It ends with a **period.** *Please sit down.*
>
> • An **exclamatory sentence** shows strong feeling.
>   It ends with an **exclamation mark.** *Hooray, I'm the winner!*
>
> • Add a **comma** and the **conjunction** *and, or,* or *but* to join parts of a
>   compound sentence. *Chaz will play violin tonight,* **or** *he will play piano.*

Underline each sentence that is written correctly.

1. When does the contest begin.

2. Oh, the music is lovely!

3. Please be on time for the show.

4. you and I can sit here.

5. Tell me all about the performance.

6. Do you see Marta and John in
   the audience?

7. Clap for all the performers

8. wow, the trumpet player was fabulous!

9. Simon wanted to come tonight, but he
   sprained his ankle playing ball.

10. We all gathered in the hallway
    during intermission.

**McGraw-Hill Language Arts**
Grade 4, Unit 1, Sentences,
pages 10–11

**10**

**At Home:** Rewrite correctly the sentences that you didn't
underline.

5

# Mixed Review

┌─ **RULES** ─────────────────────────────────────────────┐

- A **declarative sentence** makes a statement and ends in a period.

  *I like to go on picnics.*

- An **interrogative sentence** asks a question and ends in a question mark.

  *Would you like to go on a picnic?*

- An **imperative sentence** tells or asks someone to do something and ends in a period.

  *Get some hotdogs.*

- An **exclamatory sentence** shows strong feeling and ends in an exclamation point.

  *What a terrific idea!*

- Use the words *and, but,* or *or* to combine two sentences into a **compound sentence**. Use a comma before the conjunction.

  *Picnics are fun. + You have to plan them well.*

  *Picnics are fun, **but** you have to plan them well.*

└──────────────────────────────────────────────────────────┘

Circle the word that describes each kind of sentence. Add the correct end punctuation.

1. Would you like to help me plan a picnic

   declarative     interrogative     imperative     compound

2. The weather is going to be perfect

   declarative     interrogative     imperative     exclamatory

3. Call some friends and see if they can come

   declarative     interrogative     imperative     exclamatory

4. The soda was warm, but we drank it anyway

   imperative     interrogative     compound     exclamatory

5. What a perfect day

   compound     interrogative     imperative     exclamatory

**At Home:** Imagine having a family picnic. Write five sentences about it. Write one declarative, interrogative, imperative, exclamatory, and compound sentence.

**McGraw-Hill Language Arts**
**Grade 4, Unit 1, Mixed Review,**
**pages 12–13**

6

5

McGraw-Hill School Division

# Complete Subjects and Complete Predicates

**┌ RULES ═══════════════════════════════════════**

• The **complete subject** includes all the words in the subject that tell whom or what the sentence is about.

• The **complete predicate** includes all the words in the predicate that tell what the subject does or is.

*Some children read stories to others.*

complete subject     complete predicate

Tell whether the underlined part of the sentence is a complete subject or a complete predicate. Circle your answer.

1. Story Theater is a special kind of storytelling.

        complete subject          complete predicate

2. Members of the group are assigned roles.

        complete subject          complete predicate

3. The actors read their parts aloud.   complete subject     complete predicate

4. Many readers practice reading with expression.

        complete subject          complete predicate

5. They change their voices to sound like the characters.

        complete subject          complete predicate

6. Sometimes one reader is assigned only one page.

        complete subject          complete predicate

7. Many different kinds of stories can be used in Story Theater.

        complete subject          complete predicate

8. The fourth-grade class read "*The Courage of Sarah Noble.*"

        complete subject          complete predicate

9. My whole family came to the performance.

        complete subject          complete predicate

10. Our reading was a huge success.   complete subject     complete predicate

McGraw-Hill School Division

**McGraw-Hill Language Arts**
**Grade 4, Unit 1, Sentences,**
**pages 14–15**

**At Home:** Choose a story you would like to read aloud to a parent or a sibling. Read the first page aloud. Then identify the complete subject of each sentence.

# Simple Subjects

┌─ **RULES** ═══════════════════════════════════════════════
│
│ • The **complete subject** includes all the words in the subject that tell
│   whom or what the sentence is about.
│
│ • The **simple subject** is the main word in the complete
│   subject. It tells who or what the sentence is about.
│
│   **complete subject**
│        ↑
│   *At first hot <u>air</u> was used to fill big round balloons.*
│
│        **simple subject** ↑
│
└────────────────────────────────────────────────────────────

The complete subject is underlined in each sentence.
Write the simple subject on the line.

1. <u>Some inventors</u> hoped that hot-air balloons
   would become popular.                                    _____

2. <u>Many people</u> didn't think balloons should be
   used for transportation.                                 _____

3. <u>Floating in air</u> is like floating in water.        _____

4. <u>Later, propellers</u> were put on huge,
   long balloons.                                           _____

5. <u>Soon airplanes</u> proved to be faster and safer.     _____

6. <u>Today special balloons</u> are used for sport
   and to lift weather instruments.                         _____

7. <u>My parents</u> took me to an air show.                _____

8. <u>Many fantastic photographs</u>
   were on display.                                         _____

9. <u>An airplane wing</u> is curved on top
   and flat on the bottom.                                  _____

10. <u>The Wright brothers' Flyer</u> was the world's
    first successful airplane.                              _____

**At Home:** Write two sentences about things that fly.
Underline the simple subject in each sentence.

8

McGraw-Hill School Division

**McGraw-Hill Language Arts**
**Grade 4, Unit 1, Sentences,**
**pages 16–17**   10

# Simple Predicates

**RULES**

- The **complete predicate** includes all the words that tell what the subject does or is.

- The **simple predicate** is the main word in the complete predicate. It tells exactly what the subject does or is.

complete predicate

Energy <u>gives</u> things power.

simple predicate

The complete predicate is underlined in each sentence. Write the simple predicate on the line.

1. Your body <u>gets its energy from food.</u> _____

2. The energy <u>keeps you moving.</u> _____

3. Energy <u>comes from the sun.</u> _____

4. All animals <u>store energy from the sun.</u> _____

5. Moving things <u>use energy, too.</u> _____

6. A gusty wind <u>pushes a sailboat across the water.</u> _____

7. An electric current <u>flows through a wire.</u> _____

8. It <u>makes light and heat.</u> _____

9. Often, it <u>runs a machine.</u> _____

10. Electric energy <u>lights our homes.</u> _____

**McGraw-Hill Language Arts**
Grade 4, Unit 1, Sentences,
pages 18–19

10

**At Home:** Write two sentences about how you use energy. Underline the simple predicate in each sentence.

9

# Combining Sentences: Compound Subjects

---

**RULES**

- The **compound subject** is two or more simple subjects that have the same predicate. Join simple subjects with **and** or **or.**

      Ethan
      and    }→ went to the beach.
      Ginny

---

Join the subject of each sentence pair to make a compound subject. Use the word in parentheses ( ).

**1.** Some joggers run on the sand. A dog runs on the sand. (and)

_____

_____

**2.** Mom will watch Ethan swim. I will watch Ethan swim. (or)

_____

_____

**3.** Ginny collected beautiful shells.
Doug collected beautiful shells. (and)

_____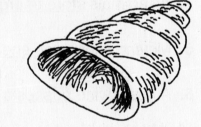

_____

_____

**4.** A pebble is in my shoe. A seashell is in my shoe. (or)

_____

_____

**5.** The chairs were set up nearby. The tables were set up nearby. (and)

_____

_____

---

**At Home:** Write a compound subject to complete this
sentence: _____*floated in the water.*

**10**

**McGraw-Hill Language Arts**
**Grade 4, Unit 1, Sentences,**
**pages 20–21**

5

McGraw-Hill School Division

# Combining Sentences: Compound Predicates

> **RULES**
> • The **compound predicate** contains two or more simple predicates that have the same subject. Join the simple predicates with **and, but,** or **or.**
>
> We <u>study and rehearse</u> our lines.
>
> Our teacher <u>laughs or cries</u> after each scene.
>
> She <u>wanted but didn't get</u> more funding.

Join the predicate of each sentence pair to make a compound predicate. Use the word in parentheses ( ).

**1.** Jeanette sings in the play. Jeanette dances in the play. (and)

_____

_____

**2.** The actors talk before the opening. The actors rest before the opening. (or)

_____

_____

**3.** The school rented chairs for the performance. The school borrowed chairs for the performance. (and)

_____

_____

**4.** My teacher didn't ask us to make costumes. My teacher persuaded us to make costumes. (but)

_____

_____

**5.** My father didn't sell 20 tickets. My father bought 20 tickets. (but)

_____

_____

# Mechanics and Usage: Correcting Run-on Sentences

> **RULES**
>
> - A **run-on sentence** contains two or more complete sentences that run together.
>
>   *A stonefish looks like a rock this disguise fools other fish.*
>
> - To fix a run-on sentence, show each complete sentence by using a capital letter and the correct end punctuation.
>
>   *A stonefish looks like a rock. This disguise fools other fish.*
>
> - You can also fix a run-on sentence by rewriting it as a compound sentence.
>
>   *A stonefish looks like a rock, and this disguise fools other fish.*

Tell which sentences are written correctly. Circle **run-on** or **correct.**

1. A stonefish never goes hungry. Its food comes right to it!    **run-on    correct**

2. Looking like a stone helps the stonefish get its food, and it also protects it from other creatures.    **run-on    correct**

3. One kind of fish looks like a clump of seaweed another looks like a piece of coral.    **run-on    correct**

4. A ferocious inhabitant of a coral reef is the moray eel it is an ugly looking creature.    **run-on    correct**

5. A four-inch-long fish swims straight to the eel. It is unaware of any danger.    **run-on    correct**

6. The little fish swims about the eel it often touches the eel.    **run-on    correct**

7. The little fish swims right into the eel's half-opened mouth then it swims out again.    **run-on    correct**

8. The ever-hungry eel did not try to eat the little fish. The eel remains perfectly still.    **run-on    correct**

9. The little fish is like a doctor, and the eel is like a patient.    **run-on    correct**

10. The little fish, called a *wrasse*, cleans the big fish it rids the big fish of tiny worms and other creatures.    **run-on    correct**

---

**At Home:** Choose a run-on sentence from above and rewrite it as two complete sentences or a compound sentence.

12

McGraw-Hill Language Arts
Grade 4, Unit 1, Sentences,
pages 24–25

10

McGraw-Hill School Division

# Mixed Review

**RULES**

- The **complete subject** includes all the words in the subject.

  *Summer camp* offers many summer activities.

- The **complete predicate** includes all the words that tell what the subject does or is.

  *Summer camp **offers many summer activities.***

- A **compound subject** has two or more simple subjects that have the same predicate. The simple subjects are joined by *and* or *or*.

  *The girls play sports.      The boys play sports.*

  *The girls **and** boys play sports.*

- A **compound predicate** has two or more simple predicates that have the same subject. The simple predicates are joined by *and, but,* or *or*.

  *The campers sleep at the camp. The campers eat at the camp.*

  *The campers sleep **and** eat at the camp.*

**A.** Underline the complete subject. Circle the complete predicate.

1. Several of my friends go to summer camp.

2. The camp provides many activities.

3. The campers learn about the wilderness.

4. A nature instructor takes them on daily field trips.

5. Several nature trails wind through the camp grounds.

**B.** Underline the compound subject or circle the compound predicate.

6. Deer and bears live on the camp grounds.

7. The campers look and listen for the animals.

8. Crafts and sports are favorite camp activities.

9. Campers design and make their own projects.

10. Parents and counselors coach sporting events.

10

**McGraw-Hill Language Arts**
**Grade 4, Unit 1, Mixed Review,**
**pages 26–27**

**At Home:** Write five sentences describing your favorite summer activity. Circle the complete subjects. Underline the complete predicates. Include one compound subject and predicate.

13

# Common Errors: Sentence Fragments and Run-on Sentences

┌─ **RULES** ─────────────────────────────────────────────────────┐

• A **sentence fragment** does not express a complete thought.

  *Have a taste of their own.       Dried grapes.*

• Correct a sentence fragment by adding a subject or a predicate.

  ***Dried fruits** have a taste of their own.     Dried grapes **are called raisins.***

• A **run-on sentence** contains two or more sentences that should stand alone.

  *Plums grow on trees dried plums are called prunes.*

• Correct a run-on sentence by rewriting it as two sentences or as a
  compound sentence.

  *Plums grow on trees. Dried plums are called prunes.*

└─────────────────────────────────────────────────────────────────┘

Read each group of words. Write *F* if it is a fragment. Write *R* if it is a run-on
sentence. Write *S* if it is a complete sentence.

_____ 1. People grow grapes many grapes are
   grown in California.

_____ 2. In warm climates.

_____ 3. Grapes grow on vines they hang on the
   vines in bunches.

_____ 4. Grapes are grown in large fields called
   vineyards.

_____ 5. Workers pick the grapes they place the
   grapes on wooden trays.

_____ 6. Placed in the sun.

_____ 7. The wooden trays stay in the sun the sun
   dries the grapes.

_____ 8. Become wrinkled and turn a blackish brown.

_____ 9. The sun dries the grapes the grapes finally
   turn into raisins.

_____10. Packed and sent to stores and sold.

McGraw-Hill School Division

---

**At Home:** Change the sentence fragments labeled above to
complete sentences or compound sentences.

14

**McGraw-Hill Language Arts**
**Grade 4, Unit 1, Sentences,**
**pages 28–29**

/10

# Study Skills: Note-Taking and Summarizing

---

- To remember what you have read, **take notes** that include enough words to help you recall important information such as the main ideas and supporting details.

- Write a **summary,** including the main topic and supporting details or facts.

---

**A.** Read the paragraph about space camp. Then underline the best choice for each item shown below.

Between the months of February and December every year, students attend the United States Space Camp in Huntsville, Alabama. The students come from the United States and countries around the world. Their interests range from math and science to engineering and space flight. They go to classes and see films about flying on the space shuttle. They also visit the space flight center. At the center, students get hands-on experience with model rockets and simulators, which allow them to become familiar with the weightlessness of space. The high point of the week-long camp is the space shuttle mission simulation, which includes launching and landing of the shuttle.

**1.** Topic:           **a.** Huntsville, Alabama

                           **b.** United States Space Camp

**2.** Main Idea:     **a.** one week between February and December

                           **b.** students learn about space shuttle flights

**3.** Supporting Detail: **a.** films, classes, visit to space flight center

                           **b.** students have different interests

**4.** Supporting Detail: **a.** people are weightless in space

                           **b.** space shuttle mission simulation with launch and landing

**B.** Write a summary about the paragraph.

**5.** _____

_____

_____

_____

_____

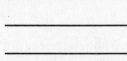

**McGraw-Hill Language Arts**
**Grade 4, Unit 1, Study Skills,**
**pages 36–37**

**At Home:** Write notes for a section of a textbook or an encyclopedia article you read. Include a topic, main idea, and supporting details.

15

# Vocabulary: Time-Order Words

---

• **Time-order words** can help you understand in what order things happen in a story. These kinds of words can help you when you are following a set of directions or learning about an event.

after afterwards this afternoon before as soon as finally first later last next meanwhile then tomorrow right now yesterday

---

Circle the time-order word that will complete each sentence correctly.

1. The (first/finally) thing this morning, Mom told me I had to clean my room.

2. (Then/Meanwhile) she told me I had to finish my homework.

3. (Tomorrow/Finally) she said I could work on my computer.

4. (Later/Now) in the day my dad asked if I wanted to play catch with him.

5. I said," (As soon as/Next) I finish this e-mail."

6. (After/Later)I signed off, I got my catcher's mitt.

7. My dad said, "I am going to give you a workout (a long time ago/ this afternoon)."

8. "Sure, sure," I teased, "just like you did (today/yesterday)."

9. "(Right now/Later) you are throwing very well," said Dad.

10. "Maybe (this morning/tomorrow) we'll work on hitting the ball."

---

**At Home:** Think about how using time-order words in directions helps you. Then write a set of directions explaining how to get from your house to school.

16

**McGraw-Hill Language Arts**
Grade 4, Unit 1, Vocabulary,
pages 38–39

10

McGraw-Hill School Division

# Composition: Main Idea

---

- A **paragraph** is a group of sentences that tell about a **main idea.** The main idea tells what the writing is about.

- A paragraph should include:
    A **topic sentence** that states the main idea.
    **Supporting details** that clarify and develop the main idea.

- To connect ideas within a paragraph, use time-order words.

- If a sentence does not contain a detail that supports the main idea, take it out.

---

For each paragraph below, the topic sentence with a main idea appears in dark type. Some of the other sentences of the paragraph contain supporting details. Other sentences contain details that do not support the main idea. Underline the detail sentences that do not support the main ideas.

**1.-2.   I found an old box yesterday.** It was lying on the floor of our attic. At first, I thought it was trash. My house has a basement and a garage. I was about to throw the old box away. Then, I heard a jiggling sound when I picked it up. So, I opened the lid. There were at least one hundred photographs of my father from long, long ago inside of the box. It's so interesting to see what he looked like when he was about my age. I called my friend to see if she wanted to come over for dinner.

**3.-4.   Stacey and I went skating on the pond yesterday.** First, our parents tested the ice to make sure it was solid and safe. In the summer, I swim in the pond. We put on our skates and took off over the ice. First, Stacey skated backwards around the rim of the pond. Next, I skated to the center of the pond and spun around like a top. Have you seen tops whose colors blur when they spin? After an hour of skating, Stacey and I collapsed, tired but happy. Finally, my mother gave us each a cup of hot cocoa from a thermos.

**5. I will never forget my first airplane ride.** The captain spoke over a loud-speaker. He welcomed everyone on board. Who invented the airplane? Then, he asked us all to put on our seat belts and make sure our seats were in their upright position. The engines roared, and the plane began to move. As the plane lifted off the runway, it felt like my heart rose up out of my body, too!

---

**McGraw-Hill Language Arts** Grade 4, Unit 1, Composition Skills, pages 40–41

**At Home:** Write a topic sentence for a paragraph that tells about the first time you did something special. Then, write sentences with three or more supporting details to complete the paragraph. **17**

# Nouns

Underline the nouns in each sentence. Then write each noun on the chart under the correct heading. Some headings will have fewer than seven nouns.

1. Mr. Finney taught history at Central School.

2. His students were encouraged to bring in interesting articles about foreign countries.

3. Usually, the teacher had an interesting historical fact to tell about the news.

4. The older children enjoyed the stories that were shared in his classroom.

5. His amusing tales usually made his listeners laugh.

| PERSONS | PLACES | THINGS |
|---|---|---|
|  |  |  |
|  |  |  |
|  |  |  |
|  |  |  |
|  |  |  |
|  |  |  |
|  |  |  |

**At Home:** Think of a sentence with nouns that are the names of a person, a place, and a thing. Write each noun in the blank spaces under the correct heading on the chart.

# Singular and Plural Nouns

```
┌─ RULES ──────────────────────────────────────────────────┐
```

- A **singular noun** names one person, place, or thing.

- A **plural noun** names two or more persons, places, or things.

- To identify **singular** or **plural nouns** it may be helpful to test a word with the questions: *Can you see one ___? Can you see two ___?*

- Add *-s* to most nouns to form the plural.

  one **boy** → two **boys**

- Add *-es* to form the plural of nouns ending in *s, x, ch,* or *sh.*

  one **bus** → two **buses**
  one **box** → two **boxes**
  one **church** → two **churches**
  one **bush** → two **bushes**

Underline the correct plural form of each noun and write it on the line.

1. cup        (cups, cupes, cupps) _____

2. plate      (plats, plaets, plates) _____

3. house      (housse, houses, houzes) _____

4. box        (boxes, boxs, boxis) _____

5. stitch     (stitchis, stitchs, stitches) _____

6. boss       (bosses, bosss, boses) _____

7. scratch    (scratched, scratches, scratchs) _____

8. bush       (busses, bushes, bushs) _____

9. light      (lights, lightes, lites) _____

10. candle    (candels, candls, candles) _____

**At Home:** Write a list of nouns that name equipment and people you might expect to find on a playground.

19

McGraw-Hill Language Arts
Grade 4, Unit 2, Nouns,
pages 90–91

10

McGraw-Hill School Division

# Nouns Ending with *y*

┌─ **RULES** ─────────────────────────────────────┐

• When forming the plural of nouns ending in *y:*

Change the *y* to *i* and add *-es* if the noun ends in a consonant + *y*.
one **baby** → two **babies**

Just add *-s* if the noun ends in a vowel + *y*.
one **day** → two **days**

└─────────────────────────────────────────────────┘

Write the correct plural noun in parentheses to complete each sentence.

1. Elliott heard that I got two new _____ last month.
   (puppys/puppies)

2. They were a special gift for my brother's and my _____.
   (birthdays/ birthdayes)

3. I had to wait several _____ before receiving my new pets.
   (Mondays, Mondais)

4. We had to travel through a few different _____ to get
   them. (citys, cities)

5. No _____ could transport us that far. (subwayes, subways)

6. We traveled on two _____ to get to the pet store and
   back. (ferrys, ferries)

7. There were several _____ of pets at the store. (varietys,
   varieties)

8. I was surprised to find some _____ there for sale.
   (monkeys, monkies)

9. My new puppies are different from the _____ I once had.
   (kittys, kitties)

10. It will take many _____ before they are properly trained.
    (daies, days)

**McGraw-Hill Language Arts**
**Grade 4, Unit 2, Nouns,**
**10** **pages 92–93**

**At Home:** Write sentences using five of the plural nouns
from the above exercise. Read your sentences aloud to a
family member.

20

# More Plural Nouns

┌─ **RULES** ─────────────────────────────────

• Some nouns do not add -s or -es to form the plural.
Some nouns have special plural forms.

  one **man** → two **men**

  one **child** → two **children**

• Some nouns have the same singular and plural forms.

  one **moose** → two **moose**

  one **deer** → two **deer**

Write the irregular plural noun from the box that completes each sentence.

| | |
|---|---|
| one woman → two women | one deer → two deer |
| one tooth → two teeth | one mouse → two mice |
| one goose → two geese | one fisherman → two fishermen |
| one scissors → two scissors | one fish → two fish |
| one foot → two feet | one trout → two trout |

1. My father helped me learn how to use a fly rod to catch _____.

2. It is a challenge to catch brook and rainbrow _____ without live bait.

3. My dad and I stood as quiet as two _____ near the edge of the stream.

4. It is impossible to go fly fishing without getting your _____ wet.

5. Most fly _____ wear special fishing boots called waders.

6. They also wear vests with pockets for small tools like pliers and _____.

7. Without scissors, they would have to bite with their _____ to cut the line.

8. Many _____ also enjoy the sport of fly fishing.

9. On our last trip, we encountered several _____ getting drinks of water.

10. We also enjoyed seeing flocks of _____ migrating overhead.

---

**At Home:** Make up a sentence for each plural noun in the chart above. Say each sentence to a parent or sibling.

**McGraw-Hill Language Arts**
**Grade 4, Unit 2, Nouns,**
**pages 94–95**

21

10

McGraw-Hill School Division

# Common and Proper Nouns

┌─ **RULES** ─────────────────────────────────────────────┐

- **Common nouns** name people, places, or things.
- **Proper nouns** name particular people, places, or things and always begin with a capital letter.

*The scientific **name** for an **animal** in **North America** is the **same** in **Europe**.*

└──────────────────────────────────────────────────────────┘

Underline common nouns and write any proper nouns that appear.

1. Red Cliff High School began classes in August, before Labor Day.

   _____

2. We learned about scientific classification in Biology 101 last November.

   _____

3. We studied that topic until the Wednesday before Thanksgiving.

   _____

4. Many centuries ago, a philosopher from Greece named Aristotle developed a

   way to classify living organisms.   _____

5. Aristotle grouped animals according to whether they had red blood.

   _____

6. A scientist named John Ray classified living organisms by their species.

   _____

7. This biologist from England noticed that members of the same species can

   breed together.   _____

8. About a century later, Carolus Linnaeus developed the classification system

   we use today.   _____

9. Linnaeus was born in the city of Kristianstad, Sweden, in 1707.

   _____

10. He first explained his system in a book titled *Species Plantarum*.

   _____

**McGraw-Hill Language Arts**
**Grade 4, Unit 2, Nouns,**
**10** **pages 96–97**

**At Home:** Write the days of the week and months of the year in order. Read your lists to a family member.

22

# Mechanics and Usage: Capitalization

```
┌─ RULES ─────────────────────────────────────────────────────────┐

• Proper nouns, including names of days, months, and holidays,
  always begin with a capital letter.
      Tuesday      February      St. Valentine's Day

• Capitalize family names that refer to specific people. Also capitalize
  titles of respect that are part of a specific name.
      Mother spoke to my teacher, Miss Meg Hargrove.

• Capitalize the first word and all important words in the title of a book,
  magazine, song, poem, play, short story, or movie.
      My favorite play is Fiddler on the Roof.

└─────────────────────────────────────────────────────────────────┘
```

Read each pair of sentences. Write the letter *C* before the sentence that is correctly written.

1. _____ Dad recently read a book to my brother Ryan called *Customs Around the World for Holidays*.

   _____ Dad recently read a book to my brother Ryan called *Customs around the World For Holidays*.

2. _____ In the United States, the last Monday in may is called memorial Day.

   _____ In the United States, the last Monday in May is called Memorial Day.

3. _____ On that day, miss lauren connolly attends a parade in Northville, michigan, with her Father and Mother.

   _____ On that day, Miss Lauren Connolly attends a parade in Northville, Michigan, with her father and mother.

4. _____ Our father once took Mother, Ryan, and me to a Thanksgiving parade.

   _____ Our Father once took mother, Ryan, and me to a thanksgiving parade.

5. _____ Mayor Frank McGinity wore an orange derby in the parade that thursday.

   _____ Mayor Frank McGinity wore an orange derby in the parade that Thursday.

**At Home:** Write a sentence that tells how your family celebrates your favorite holiday.

23

McGraw-Hill School Division

**McGraw-Hill Language Arts**
**Grade 4, Unit 2, Nouns,**
**pages 98–99**

5

# Mixed Review

---

**RULES**

- A **singular noun** names only one person, place, or thing.

  person           thing         place

  *A **friend** of mine formed a **club** in my **neighborhood**.*

- A **plural noun** names more than one person, place, or thing. Add **-s** to form the plural of most nouns.

  *My friends and I are interested in outer space.*

- Add **-es** to form the plural of nouns ending in *s, x, ch,* or *sh.*

  *speech + es = speeches*      *class + es = classes*

- To form the plural of nouns ending with a consonant and *y,* change the *y* to *i* and add **-es.**   *family − y + i + es = families*

- A **proper noun** is a noun that names a particular person, place, or thing. A proper noun always begins with a capital letter.

  **common nouns:** *teacher*     *city*
  **proper nouns:**    *Mr. Jarvis*    *Houston*

---

**A.** Circle the correct form of the plural noun in parentheses.

1. We have been studying the (galaxys, galaxies).

2. Several (country, countries) want to work together to study outer space.

3. There are many (branchs, branches) of space science.

4. In some (citys, cities) there are huge telescopes to look at the stars.

5. Some (friends, friendes) in my neighborhood formed a star club.

**B.** Write the proper noun(s) in each sentence and capitalize them.

6. Mrs. dunne teaches us about space. _____

7. She told us about a huge telescope in california. _____

8. It is at the palomar observatory. _____

9. The telescope was designed by george hale. _____

10. He was an american astronomer. _____

McGraw-Hill Language Arts
Grade 4, Unit 2, Mixed Review,
pages 100–101    10

**At Home:** Look at the night sky with a family member. Write five sentence about what you see. Include some singular, plural, and proper nouns. Circle all the nouns you use.    24

# Singular Possessive Nouns

> **RULES**
>
> - A **singular possessive noun** is a word that shows that something belongs to one person or thing.
>
>   *the* **cell's** *shape (the shape belongs to one cell)*
>   *the* **plant's** *leaves (the leaves belong to one plant)*
>
> - Usually, make a singular noun possessive by adding an **apostrophe** with the letter **s** to a singular noun.
>
>   <u>*The fur of an animal*</u> *is made up of cells.*
>
>   **animal + 's = animal's**
>
>   *An* **animal's** <u>*fur*</u> *is made up of cells.*

Rewrite each sentence using a singular possessive noun to replace some of the words in each underlined phrase.

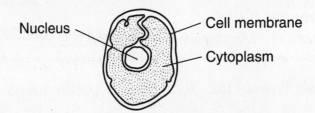

Nucleus — Cell membrane
— Cytoplasm

1. The <u>cells of the body</u> breathe, take in food, and eliminate wastes.

   _____

2. The nucleus in the center of a cell is the <u>control point of the cell</u>.

   _____

3. A <u>purpose of the cell membrane</u> is to hold the cell together.

   _____

4. You can see cells using the <u>microscope of the school</u>.

   _____

5. The <u>nervous system of the body</u> is made up of branched nerve cells.

   _____

**At Home:** Write sentences telling about three items owned by different members of your family.

25

McGraw-Hill School Division

**McGraw-Hill Language Arts**
**Grade 4, Unit 2, Nouns,**
**pages 102–103**

5

# Plural Possessive Nouns

**RULES**

- A **plural possessive noun** is a word that shows something belongs to two or more persons or things.
  *the **officials' plans*** (the plans belong to more than one official)
- When a plural noun ends in *s*, add an **apostrophe (')** to form the plural possessive noun. If the plural noun does not end in *-s*, add an **apostrophe** and *-s* **('s).**
  *the **brothers' baseball gloves**   **women's** sports*

Write the letter **C** next to the phrase that has the same meaning as the underlined words in the sentence.

1. <u>Groups of students</u> will do volunteer work.

   _____ groups' students

   _____ students' groups

2. The <u>purposes of the groups</u> will be to improve our community.

   _____ groups' purposes

   _____ group's purposes

3. <u>The reasons of my friends</u> for volunteering are admirable.

   _____ my friends' reasons

   _____ my friend's reasons

4. Some of the <u>reasons of other children</u> are different.

   _____ other children's reasons

   _____ other childrens' reasons

5. All the <u>members of the clubs</u> are anxious to begin their projects.

   _____ members' clubs

   _____ clubs' members

6. Some students will need <u>the permission of both parents</u>.

   _____ both parents' permission

   _____ both parent's permission

7. Work will be done under the <u>supervision of teachers</u>.

   _____ teacher's supervision

   _____ teachers' supervision

8. The principal requested <u>cooperation of people</u> at school.

   _____ people's cooperation

   _____ cooperation's people

9. Many <u>citizens of the neighborhoods</u> will benefit from our work.

   _____ neighborhoods' citizens

   _____ neighborhood's citizens

10. They will enjoy the <u>benefits of the improvements</u>.

    _____ benefits' improvements

    _____ improvements' benefits

**McGraw-Hill Language Arts** Grade 4, Unit 2, Nouns, pages 104–105   **At Home:** Rewrite five of the above sentences using the correct plural possessive noun.   10   26

McGraw-Hill School Division

# Combining Sentences: Nouns

┌─ **RULES** ─────────────────────────────────

• You can combine sentences that have similar ideas by joining two nouns with the conjunctions *and* or *or*.

**Combine nouns in the subject:**
*Andrea works at the library.*
*James works at the library.* ⟍⟶ **Andrea and James** *work at the library.*

**Combine nouns in the predicate:**
*You can borrow books.*
*You can borrow tapes.* ⟍⟶ *You can borrow* **books or tapes.**

└─────────────────────────────────────────────

Combine each pair of sentences using the word in parentheses.

1. Do you want to borrow books? Do you want to borrow periodicals? (or)

_____

2. Librarians are helpful for finding information. Card catalogs are helpful for finding information. (and)

_____

3. Library catalogs can be found on cards. Library catalogs can be found on computers. (or)

_____

4. The card catalog lists hardbound books. The card catalog lists paperback books. (and)

_____

5. Is your research for work? Is your research for school? (or)

_____

**At Home:** Underline the nouns that can be combined in each pair of sentences above.

**McGraw-Hill Language Arts**
**Grade 4, Unit 2, Nouns,**
**pages 106–107**

27

5

McGraw-Hill School Division

# Mechanics and Usage: Abbreviations

> **RULES**
>
> Most titles of people, days of the week, and months of the year can be made into a shorter form called an **abbreviation**.
>
> • Begin abbreviations with a **capital letter.**
>
> • End abbreviations with a **period.**
>
> | Titles | Days | Months |
> |---|---|---|
> | Mr. → Mister | Mon. → Monday | Jan. → January |
> | Dr. → Doctor | Wed. → Wednesday | Mar. → March |
> | Sen. → Senator | Thurs. → Thursday | Sept. → September |
> | Gov. → Governor | Sun. → Sunday | Nov. → November |

Circle the correct abbreviation for the underlined word and rewrite the phrase on the line.

1. a <u>Saturday</u> book club      Satur.      S.D.      Sat.

_____

2. <u>Mister</u> and Mrs. King      Mr.      Miss      Msr.

_____

3. meeting in <u>January</u>      Ja.      Jun.      Jan.

_____

4. lecture by <u>Doctor</u> Bond      Drs.      Dr.      Doc.

_____

5. program about <u>Senator</u> McCord      Str.      Sentr.      Sen.

_____

**McGraw-Hill Language Arts**
**Grade 4, Unit 2, Nouns,**
pages 108–109

5

**At Home:** Write all the days of the week and their abbreviations in the order they appear on the calendar.

28

# Mixed Review

┌─ **RULES** ─────────────────────────────────────────────────┐

- To make a singular noun possessive, add an **apostrophe** and **-s.**

  *theater* + ' + *s* = *theater's*    *actors* + ' = *actors'*

- To make a plural noun that ends in *s* possessive, add an **apostrophe.**

- To make a plural noun that does not end in *s* possessive, add an **apostrophe** and **-s.**

  *women* + ' + *s* = *women's*

- You can **combine sentences** by joining two nouns with *and* or *or.*

  *The theater had one floor. The theater had a balcony.*

  *The theater had one floor and a balcony.*

└─────────────────────────────────────────────────────────────┘

**A.** Write the correct possessive form of each noun in parentheses.

1. (men) The _____ chorus is very talented.

2. (magician) The _____ show is very clever.

3. (children) The _____ acts are very cute.

4. (dancers) The _____ costumes are very colorful.

5. (singer) The _____ song was very beautiful.

**B.** Join two nouns with *and* or *or* to combine each pair of sentences.

6. I bought tickets. I bought programs.

   _____

7. The costumes were very imaginative. The sets were very imaginative.

   _____

8. The theater had new seats. The theater had new lounges.

   _____

9. The snack bar served sandwiches. The snack bar served drinks.

   _____

10. The musicians were great. The actors were great.

    _____

McGraw-Hill School Division

# Common Errors: Plurals and Possessives

┌─ **RULES** ────────────────────────────────

A **plural noun** names more than one person, place, or thing.
Most plural nouns are formed by adding **-s** or **-es.**

lamb**s**          fox**es**

A **possessive noun** shows who or what owns or has something.

• A **singular possessive noun** is formed by adding **-'s.**

cat + 's          cat's  whiskers

• A **plural possessive noun** that ends in **-s** is formed by adding **'.**

dogs + '          dogs'  paws

• A **plural possessive noun** that does not end in **-s** is formed by adding **-'s.**

mice + 's          mice's  tails

└────────────────────────────────────────────

Write the possessive form of each underlined noun.

1. the zoo for <u>children</u>        _____ zoo

2. the skin of a <u>snake</u>        _____ skin

3. the fur of <u>foxes</u>        _____ fur

4. the feathers of <u>geese</u>        _____ feathers

5. the horns of a <u>goat</u>        _____ horns

6. the claws of an <u>eagle</u>        _____ claws

7. the tails of <u>monkeys</u>        _____ tails

8. the spines on <u>hedgehogs</u>        _____ spines

9. the hooves on a <u>pony</u>        _____ hooves

10. the beaks on <u>parrots</u>        _____ beaks

**McGraw-Hill Language Arts** Grade 4, Unit 2, Nouns, pages 112–113

**At Home:** Write three sentences describing your favorite kind of animal. Include a possessive noun in each sentence.

30

# Study Skills: Parts of a Book

Certain parts of a book help you find information quickly.

In the front of a book you may find:

• a **title page** with the title, author, and the publisher of the book.
• a **copyright page** with the date the book was published.
• a **table of contents** listing the titles of chapters and the page numbers on which they begin.

In the back of a book you may find:

• a **glossary** with the spelling, pronunciation, and definition of important words in the book.
• an **index** with an alphabetical listing of all the topics in the book and the page numbers on which they can be found.

Look at the pages from a nonfiction book. On the line below each page, identify whether the page is a *title page, copyright page, table of contents, glossary,* or *index.*

| | | |
|---|---|---|
| **Z**<br>**zygote** (zī´gōt)<br>Developing individual produced from germ cells. | **All About the Cell**<br>by D. Ortega<br><br>Elsa Saldor Publishers, Inc.<br>San Diego • Chicago •<br>New York | Chapter 10<br>Cell Studies and<br>Medicine . . . . . . . . .89<br>Chapter 11<br>Cell Research and the<br>Foods We Eat . . . . .101<br>Chapter 12<br>Research for the<br>Future . . . . . . . . . .106 |

1. _____   2. _____   3. _____

| | |
|---|---|
| © 2001<br>All rights reserved.<br>Elsa Saldor Publishers, Inc.<br>100 Union Square<br>New York, New York 10000<br>Printed in the United States of America<br>ISBN 0-01—000034-1/2 | Microscope, 53<br>Mitochondria, 5, 89–91<br>Mitosis,<br>  definition, 27<br>  phases of cell division<br>          40–42<br>Molecular Biology, 65<br>Nucleus, 4, 33, 78, 99 |

4. _____   5. _____

# Vocabulary: Compound Words

> • A compound word is a word made from two or more smaller words that
> are joined together.
>
> **brain + storm = brainstorm**      **down + stairs = downstairs**

**A.** Underline the compound word or words in each sentence. Put a diagonal
line (/) between the smaller words that make up the compound word.

1. I wear my backpack to school every day. _____

2. I also carry my lunchbox to school. _____

3. When I go to a football game, I pack a sandwich and a thermos with a hot

   drink. _____

4. After school, I swap trading cards with my classmates. _____

5. On Saturday afternoon, I usually visit Granny, who gives me homemade

   cookies. _____

**B.** Choose words from the word box to complete each compound word in a
sentence.

| row | sand | sea | some | star | summer |
|-----|------|-----|------|------|--------|

6. I love the _____ time when we can go to the beach.

7. I help my little brother build _____ castles.

8. We found a beautiful _____ fish that had washed ashore.

9. We always collect _____ shells that we can paint.

10. Dad takes us fishing in a _____ boat.

10 **McGraw-Hill Language Arts**
**Grade 4, Unit 2, Vocabulary,**
**pages 122–123**

**At Home:** Choose words from the word box and make up
other compound words. Read your list to a family member.

32

# Composition: Writing Descriptions

- A good **description** is a vivid picture you create with words. Your word picture makes the reader feel like he or she knows the person, place, thing, or idea you are writing about.

- Put the pieces of the description together in logical order, such as from top to bottom or from side to side.

- In your description, include words and details that connect with a reader's sense of sight, smell, sound, taste, or touch.

| **sense of sound** | **sense of smell** |
|---|---|
| *The siren hurt my ears.* | *The room smells like sweet vanilla.* |

On the line, write the sense described in each sentence: *sight, smell, touch, taste, sound.*

1. The baby squealed like a happy piglet. _____

2. The sour candy made my lips pucker. _____

3. Henry could sniff the smoke from the campfire. _____

4. The palace blinded me with dazzling gold decorations. _____

5. The wet sand felt like cool velvet. _____

6. The train ahead of us groaned like a hurt animal. _____

7. The bacon sizzled on the griddle. _____

8. Blooming flowers filled the air with sweet perfume. _____

9. The wind whipped my hair right to left across my cheeks. _____

10. The scent of baking cookies lured us into the kitchen. _____

**At Home:** What do your five senses tell you? Name each sense and tell how it helps you.

33

**McGraw-Hill Language Arts**
**Grade 4, Unit 2, Composition Skills,**
**pages 124–125** /10

McGraw-Hill School Division

## Action Verbs

┌─ **RULES** ─────────────────────────────────────────────┐

• An **action verb** is a verb that expresses action.

• An **action verb** tells what the subject does or did.

   *Marsha **paints** pictures as a hobby.*

   *Marsha **draws** pictures as a hobby.*

   *Marsha **sketches** pictures as a hobby.*

└─────────────────────────────────────────────────────────┘

Write the action verb in each sentence.

1. Marsha taught herself how to paint. _____

2. She read many books about painting. _____

3. She watched television shows about painting. _____

4. She even talked to a few painters. _____

5. Now Marsha paints whenever she can. _____

6. She often makes sketches of animals. _____

7. Sometimes she exhibits her paintings at art shows. _____

8. She won several prizes for her work at the last show. _____

9. Several people commented on her paintings. _____

10. She even sold two of her paintings to complete strangers. _____

McGraw-Hill School Division

**McGraw-Hill Language Arts**
**Grade 4, Unit 3, Verbs,**
pages 170–171
10

**At Home:** Write three sentences about something you like to do. Include an action verb in each sentence. Circle each action verb you write.

34

# Verb Tenses

---

**RULES**

The tense of a verb tells you if something takes place in the present, in the past, or in the future.

- A verb in the **present tense** tells what happens now.
- A verb in the **past tense** tells what has already happened.
- A verb in the **future tense** tells what is going to happen.
  To write the future tense, use the special verb *will.*

| Present Tense | Past Tense | Future Tense |
|---|---|---|
| Insects <u>survive</u> almost everywhere. | They <u>survived</u> millions of years ago. | They <u>will survive</u> in the future. |

---

Circle whether the underlined verb is in the present, past, or future tense.

1. Our science teacher <u>decided</u> to teach about insects.
   present         past         future

2. She <u>told</u> us about the different kinds of insects.
   present         past         future

3. We <u>will spend</u> several days learning about them.
   present         past         future

4. The class <u>divides</u> into small groups.
   present         past         future

5. Each group <u>chooses</u> a kind of insect to study.
   present         past         future

6. At the end of the week, each group <u>will make</u> a presentation.
   present         past         future

7. The class <u>will take</u> a field trip to see a museum exhibit.
   present         past         future

8. The museum exhibit <u>shows</u> hundreds of kinds of insects.
   present         past         future

9. Everyone <u>voted</u> in favor of taking the trip.
   present         past         future

10. Afterward, the class <u>will discuss</u> what they saw.
    present         past         future

---

**At Home:** Write three sentences about a favorite topic. Write one sentence in the present tense, one in the past tense, and one in the future tense.

**35**

McGraw-Hill Language Arts
Grade 4, Unit 3, Verbs,
pages 172–173

`10`

McGraw-Hill School Division

# Subject-Verb Agreement

Write the correct form of the verb in parentheses.

1. Chen _____ picture postcards. (collect)

2. He _____ his collection in special albums. (keep)

3. The cards _____ him of places he has been. (remind)

4. He _____ cards for his collection on family trips. (buy)

5. Most of the cards _____ scenes from the Southwest. (show)

6. Chen often _____ there with his family. (visit)

7. Several cards _____ scenes of the Grand Canyon. (include)

8. Chen often _____ he could visit there again. (wish)

9. Sometimes people _____ Chen picture postcards. (send)

10. He _____ them to his collection. (add)

McGraw-Hill School Division

**McGraw-Hill Language Arts**
**Grade 4, Unit 3, Verbs,**
**pages 174–175**

10

**At Home:** Use a newspaper article to find two sentences with plural subjects and two sentences with singular subjects. Copy each sentence. Underline each subject. Circle each verb.

# Spelling Present-Tense and Past-Tense Verbs

┌─ **RULES** ─────────────────────────────────┐

**Spelling Rules for Adding *-es* or *-ed* to Some Verbs**

- Change the *y* to *i* before adding *-es* or *-ed* to verbs that end with a consonant and *y*.

  ***carry*** = *carries* or *carried*

- Double the final consonant before adding *-ed* to one-syllable verbs that end with one vowel followed by one consonant.

  ***trim*** = *trimmed*

- Drop the *e* before adding *-es* or *-ed* to verbs that end in *e*.

  ***smile*** = *smiles* or *smiled*

└────────────────────────────────────────────┘

Write the correct present-tense or past-tense form of each verb in parentheses.

1. Cody (shop) for a new camera. *present* _____
2. Last week he (stop) at several stores. *past* _____
3. They all (carry) many kinds of cameras. *present* _____
4. Cody (know) the special features of each kind. *present* _____
5. He (remove) a camera from its case. *past* _____
6. He (worry) that it was too large and heavy. *past* _____
7. He (try) out another one with a zoom lens. *past* _____
8. Cody (decide) to buy it. *past* _____
9. He (hurry) home to try it out. *past* _____
10. That afternoon he (snap) pictures of everything. *past* _____

**At Home:** Look through a book you have read. Find five sentences with present-tense verbs. Find five sentences with past-tense verbs. List the verbs under the headings *Present Tense* and *Past Tense*.

**McGraw-Hill Language Arts**
**Grade 4, Unit 3, Verbs,**
**pages 176–177** | 10 |

McGraw-Hill School Division

# Mechanics and Usage: Commas in a Series

┌─ **RULES** ─────────────────────────────────

- A **comma** tells the reader to pause between the words that it separates.

- Use commas to separate items in a series of three or more words.

- Do not use a comma after the last word in a series.

  Ted │,│ Peter │,│ Rosa │,│ and Nora │ │ are neighbors.

└────────────────────────────────────────────

Rewrite each sentence. Use commas where they are needed.

1. Ted Peter Rosa and Nora made a garden together.

   _____

2. They had to buy a rake a shovel and a hoe.

   _____

3. Rosa and Peter raked up rocks twigs and litter.

   _____

4. Ted and Nora dug turned and raked the soil.

   _____

5. Together they decided to plant beans tomatoes carrots and corn.

   _____

6. They planted petunias sunflowers and daisies along the edge.

   _____

7. Sun rain and care helped things grow quickly.

   _____

8. The friends took turns weeding hoeing and watering.

   _____

9. Soon they were picking cooking and eating things from the garden.

   _____

10. Making the garden was enjoyable successful and practical.

    _____

**McGraw-Hill Language Arts**
**Grade 4, Unit 3, Verbs,**
**pages 178–179**
10

**At Home:** Write about something you have done with friends. Include at least three sentences that have a series of three or more words.

38

McGraw-Hill School Division

# Mixed Review

┌─ **RULES** ─────────────────────────────────────────┐

• Action verbs in the **present tense** tell what is happening now.

• Action verbs in the **past tense** tell what happened in the past.

• Action verbs in the **future tense** tell what will happen in the future.

• Add *-s* to most present-tense verbs if the subject is singular. Add *-es* to verbs that end in *s, ch, sh, x,* or *z.* Do not add *-s* or *-es* if the subject is plural or *I* or *you.*

• For verbs ending in a consonant and *y,* change the *y* to *i* before adding *-es* or *-ed.*

• For one-syllable verbs ending in one vowel and one consonant, double the consonant before adding *-ed.*

• For verbs ending in *e,* drop the *e* before adding *-ed.*

└──────────────────────────────────────────────────┘

**A.** Circle the correct tense of the underlined verb.

1. My father <u>learned</u> to play the piano at an early age.   **present   past   future**

2. He <u>enjoys</u> playing the piano for friends.   **present   past   future**

3. Practice <u>will make</u> him even better than he is now.   **present   past   future**

4. I <u>like</u> to listen to guitar music on the radio.   **present   past   future**

5. Someday I <u>will take</u> guitar lessons.   **present   past   future**

**B.** Write the verb in parentheses ( ) that completes each sentence.

6. Two of my friends (play, plays) musical instruments. _____

7. Marta (take, takes) piano lessons every week.   _____

8. John (practice, practices) the saxophone.   _____

9. My parents (want, wants) me to learn how to play.   _____

10. It (amaze, amazes) me when I see people playing music.   _____

**At Home:** Find out if someone in your family plays a musical instrument. Write a paragraph about it. Include some verbs in the present, past, and future tense.

39

McGraw-Hill Language Arts
Grade 4, Unit 3, Mixed Review,
pages 180–181   10

# Main Verbs and Helping Verbs

---

**RULES**

- The **main verb** is the most important verb in a sentence. It tells what the subject does or is.

  *The puppet show will **begin** in an hour.*

- A **helping verb** is a verb that comes before the main verb. It helps the main verb show an action or make a statement.

  *The puppet show **will** begin in an hour.*

| Helping Verbs |
| :---: |
| *am, is, are, was, were, has, have, had, will* |

---

Read each sentence.
Write the helping verb in
the first column and the
main verb in the second column.

1. A theater group was
   performing a puppet show. _____ _____

2. The puppets were dressed
   in colorful costumes. _____ _____

3. The puppet theater was
   designed like an ancient castle. _____ _____

4. The puppets are attached
   to strings. _____ _____

5. The puppeteers were standing
   above the puppet theater. _____ _____

6. They will work the strings to
   bring the puppets to life. _____ _____

7. They are using a different
   voice for each character. _____ _____

8. The children are watching
   in amazement. _____ _____

9. Even the adults were enjoying
   themselves. _____ _____

10. The puppets had won
    everyone's admiration. _____ _____

**McGraw-Hill Language Arts**
**Grade 4, Unit 3, Verbs,**
**pages 182–183**

`10`

**At Home:** Write three sentences about something interesting you have watched. Include a helping verb and a main verb in each sentence.

**40**

# Using Helping Verbs

┌─ **RULES** ─────────────────────────────────────────────────┐

• *Has, have,* and *had* are helping verbs. You can use them with the past-tense form of a verb to show an action that has already happened.

Use *has* with a singular subject and *he, she,* or *it.*

> My sister **has sailed** on a boat.
> She **has sailed** many times.

Use *have* with plural subjects and *I, you, we,* or *they.*

> Many people **have sailed** on the ocean.
> I **have sailed** on the lake.

Use *had* with singular or plural subjects.

> My friend **had sailed** last summer.
> My friends **had sailed** at camp.

└────────────────────────────────────────────────────────────┘

Write the correct form of the helping verb in parentheses.

1. Whale watching _____ attracted many tourists. (have, has)

2. Many people _____ enjoyed the thrill of seeing whales. (have, has)

3. My friends and I _____ decided to go whale watching. (have, has)

4. The boat _____ sailed several times that day. (have, had)

5. On the first trip, the passengers _____ spotted many whales. (has, had)

6. The whales _____ discovered a good feeding area. (have, has)

7. The boat's captain _____ sighted them not far away. (have, had)

8. One whale _____ surfaced beside the boat. (have, has)

9. A few whales _____ leaped into the air. (has, had)

10. Now they _____ crashed back into the water. (have, has)

**At Home:** Find a picture in a magazine that you like. Write three sentences about it. Use the helping verbs *have, has,* or *had* in each sentence.

McGraw-Hill Language Arts
Grade 4, Unit 3, Verbs,
pages 184–185 / 10

McGraw-Hill School Division

# Linking Verbs

**RULES**

- An **action verb** tells what the subject does or did.

  *Nocturnal animals* **sleep** *during the day.*

- A **linking verb** links the subject of a sentence to a noun or adjective in the predicate. A linking verb does not express action.

  *Nocturnal animals* **are** *creatures of the night.*

- The words **am, is, are, was,** and **were** are important linking verbs. They are forms of the verb **be**.

Tell whether each underlined verb is an action verb or a linking verb. Write your answer.

1. Nocturnal animals <u>are</u> nighttime creatures. _____

2. They <u>sleep</u> during most of the day. _____

3. Bats <u>are</u> nocturnal animals. _____

4. They <u>live</u> in caves during the day. _____

5. They <u>hunt</u> for food during the night. _____

6. Bats <u>are</u> the only mammals that can fly. _____

7. There <u>are</u> more than 900 kinds of bats. _____

8. I <u>am</u> one of their greatest fans. _____

9. Once I <u>was</u> at the entrance to a bat cave. _____

10. At dusk, the bats <u>flew</u> out of the cave. _____

11. It <u>was</u> a terrific and awesome sight. _____

12. One large bat <u>is</u> the flying fox. _____

13. It <u>makes</u> its home in tropical forests. _____

14. Brown bats <u>are</u> much smaller. _____

15. They <u>inhabit</u> many parts of the United States. _____

**McGraw-Hill Language Arts**
Grade 4, Unit 3, Verbs,
pages 186–187

15

**At Home:** Read a paragraph from a magazine or newspaper article to a family member. Identify any linking verbs you see.

42

# Using Linking Verbs

**RULES**

• *Am, is,* and *are* are **present-tense linking verbs.** They must agree with the subject of the sentence. Subjects can be singular or plural.
**Singular:** *I, he, she, it*    **Plural:**    *you, we, they*
   *She **is** a musician. (singular)*      *You **are** musicians. (plural)*

• *Was* and *were* are **past-tense linking verbs.** They must agree with the subject of the sentence. Subjects can be singular or plural.
   *She **was** a musician. (singular)*    *They **were** musicians. (plural)*

Rewrite the sentence with the correct form of the linking verb in parentheses.

1. Anita (is, are) a member of the orchestra.

_____

2. Orchestras (is, are) large groups of musicians.

_____

3. Anita (is, were) one of the violin players.

_____

4. I (am, were) one of the cellists.

_____

5. Last year our concerts (was, were) very popular.

_____

6. Our conductor (was, were) Mr. Ortez.

_____

7. All of our musicians (is, are) first rate.

_____

8. They (are, was) wonderful when they play together.

_____

9. Everyone (is, were) very proud to be a member.

_____

10. Our first concert this year (was, were) a huge success.

_____

**At Home:** Write three sentences about music. Use linking verbs in each sentence.

43

**McGraw-Hill Language Arts**
**Grade 4, Unit 3, Verbs,**
**pages 188–189**  /10

# Irregular Verbs

┌─ **RULES** ─────────────────────────────────────────┐

- You do not always add **-ed** to form the past tense of verbs. Verbs that do not add **-ed** to form the past tense are called **irregular verbs.**

- Most irregular verbs change their spelling to form the past tense.

    Here are some examples.

| Verb | Past | Past with has, have, or had |
|------|------|------------------------------|
| go | went | gone |
| do | did | done |
| see | saw | seen |
| run | ran | run |
| come | came | come |
| give | gave | given |
| sing | sang | sung |
| eat | ate | eaten |
| make | made | made |
| bring | brought | brought |

└─────────────────────────────────────────────────────┘

Write the correct past tense form of the verb in parentheses.

1. Rosa and Luis had (go) _____ to the wild animal park.

2. They have (see) _____ some of the exhibits before.

3. Some of the animals (come) _____ out to play.

4. Monkeys (run) _____ through an artificial rain forest.

5. The large cats (give) _____ a roaring performance.

6. The elephants (make) _____ loud trumpeting sounds.

7. Rosa and Luis had (bring) _____ a picnic lunch with them.

8. They (eat) _____ it near the tropical bird exhibit.

9. Some of the birds (sing) _____ unfamiliar songs.

10. Rosa and Luis had (do) _____ this before.

**10** **McGraw-Hill Language Arts**
**Grade 4, Unit 3, Verbs,**
**pages 190–191**

**At Home:** Write about something you have done with friends. Include at least three sentences that use irregular verbs in the past tense.

44

# More Irregular Verbs

┌─ **RULES** ─────────────────────────────────────────────┐

- **Irregular** verbs do not add **-ed** to form the past tense. Instead, the spelling of an irregular verb changes.

| Verb | Past | Past with has, have, or had |
|------|------|------------------------------|
| begin | began | begun |
| draw | drew | drawn |
| drive | drove | driven |
| fly | flew | flown |
| grow | grew | grown |
| ride | rode | ridden |
| swim | swam | swum |
| take | took | taken |
| throw | threw | thrown |
| write | wrote | written |

└──────────────────────────────────────────────────────────┘

Circle the correct form of the verb in parentheses.

1. My family has (did, done) many interesting things.

2. My brother (fly, flew) in a helicopter.

3. My sister has (swam, swum) in many swimming meets.

4. I have (rode, ridden) in bicycle marathons.

5. My mom has (drew, drawn) pictures of us.

6. My dad (began, begun) to take flying lessons.

7. My grandfather has (driven, drove) race cars.

8. My grandmother (wrote, written) a book.

9. My parents have (took, taken) dancing lessons.

10. My uncle has (grew, grown) prize-winning roses.

McGraw-Hill School Division

**At Home:** Write three sentences about something you used to do when you were younger. Use an irregular verb in each sentence.

45

**McGraw-Hill Language Arts**
**Grade 4, Unit 3, Verbs,**
**pages 192–193**

10

# Mechanics and Usage: Contractions with *Not*

**RULES**

- A **contraction** is a shortened form of two words. An **apostrophe (')** takes the place of one or more letters that are left out. Several contractions are made by combining a verb and the word **_not._**

**does + not = does + n't = doesn't**

| is not | isn't | has not | hasn't |
|---|---|---|---|
| are not | aren't | have not | haven't |
| was not | wasn't | had not | hadn't |
| were not | weren't | do not | don't |
| will not | won't | did not | didn't |

**A.** Draw lines to match the contractions and the words.

**1.** was not                     aren't

**2.** has not                     isn't

**3.** do not                      wasn't

**4.** will not                     won't

**5.** have not                    doesn't

**6.** does not                    hasn't

**7.** is not                       haven't

**8.** did not                      weren't

**9.** are not                      didn't

**10.** were not                   don't

**B.** Write the two words that make up each contraction in parentheses.

**11.** I (haven't) _____ seen a purple sky.

**12.** I (don't) _____ have green hair.

**13.** Trees (aren't) _____ blue and gold.

**14.** A car (doesn't) _____ talk to you.

**15.** I (won't) _____ ever see a cow that flies.

**McGraw-Hill Language Arts**
**Grade 4, Unit 3, Verbs,**
**pages 194–195**

**At Home:** Read an article in a newspaper or magazine.
Make a list of all the contractions you find.

# Mixed Review

┌─ **RULES** ─────────────────────────────────────────────────┐

- The **main verb** in a sentence shows what a subject does or is. It is the most important verb.

  *I **acted** in the class play.*

- A **helping verb** comes before the main verb. It helps the main verb show an action or make a statement.

  *I **had** learned my lines well.*

- A **linking verb** links the subject of a sentence to a noun or adjective in the predicate. A linking verb does not express action.

  *The play **was** a great success.*

**Helping Verbs**
*am, is, are, was, were, has, have, had, will*

**Linking Verbs**
*am, is, are, was, were*

└─────────────────────────────────────────────────────────────┘

Draw one line under each main verb. Draw two lines under each helping verb. Circle each linking verb.

1. I am a member of the class play.

2. Many of my friends are in the play, too.

3. We have written our own play to perform.

4. My friend Jill is the lead character.

5. She has learned all her lines well.

6. The cast has rehearsed many times.

7. Our teacher has helped us every night.

8. She thinks we are doing a great job.

9. The costumes and props will surprise everyone.

10. Putting on a play is a hard job.

**At Home:** Write a paragraph about a movie or television show you have watched. Use main, helping, and linking verbs.

47

**McGraw-Hill Language Arts**
**Grade 4, Unit 3, Mixed Review,**
**pages 196–197** / 10

McGraw-Hill School Division

# Common Errors: Subject-Verb Agreement

┌─ **RULES** ─────────────────────────────────────────────┐

• When parts of a compound subject are joined by ***and,*** use a ***plural verb.***

*Juan and Mario* **play** *trumpets.*

• When the parts of a compound subject are joined by ***or,*** the verb agrees with the subject that is closer to it.

*Songs or a dance* **begins** *the show.*

*Either a table or trays* **hold** *snacks.*

• When a verb ends with a consonant and ***y,*** change the ***y*** to ***i*** and add ***-es*** to form a singular verb. *fly → flies*

• When a verb ends with a vowel and ***y,*** add ***-s*** to form a singular verb. Do not change the spelling of the verb. *spray → sprays*

└────────────────────────────────────────────────────────┘

Complete each sentence. Write the verb in parentheses ( ) that agrees with the compound subject of each sentence.

1. The music class or art club _____ having a talent show. (is, are)

2. The girls and boys _____ variety acts. (presents, present)

3. Linda and Kelly _____ a duet. (sings, sing)

4. My sister and brother _____ bicycle tricks. (performs, perform)

5. Either Mark or Shelly _____ magic tricks. (do, does)

6. Either my teacher or her husband _____ the guitar. (plays, play)

7. Taki and Miko _____ together on the piano. (plays, play)

8. My family and friends _____ in the audience. (sits, sit)

9. Cheers or applause _____ from everywhere. (comes, come)

10. Both performers and audience _____ the show. (enjoys, enjoy)

**McGraw-Hill Language Arts**
**Grade 4, Unit 3, Verbs,**
**pages 198–199**
10

**At Home:** Write three sentences about the talents you or family members have. Include compound subjects in each sentence.

48

McGraw-Hill School Division

# Study Skills: Card Catalog

- Use the alphabetically arranged **card catalog** to locate a book in the library. You will find it in a set of drawers or on a computer.
- Look at the **author cards, title cards,** or **subject cards** in the card catalog. Each kind of card gives the same information in a different order.
- Use the **call number** on the upper-left part of the card. Each kind of card for the same book shows the same call number.

629.8
D
    D'Ignazio, Fred
    Working Robots.
New York: Lodestar Books, © 1982.
149 p.: illus.

629.45
M
    Animals in Orbit.
    McGlade Marko, Katherine
New York: Franklin Watts, © 1991.
61 p.: illus.

629.44    SPACE
C
    Cross, Wilbur and Susanna
    Space Shuttle.
Chicago: Children's Press, © 1988.
134 p.: illus.

The **author card** lists the author's last name first.

The **title card** shows the title first.

The **subject card** begins with the subject of the book.

Use the sample catalog cards above to answer each question.

1. What is the title of the book about space? _____
2. Who wrote the book *Animals in Orbit*? _____
3. In what year was the book *Animals in Orbit* published? _____
4. How many of the books have illustrations? _____
5. Which of the three books has the most pages? _____
6. Which book has a title card on this page? _____
7. What is the call number of the book about the space shuttle? _____
8. In what year was the book *Working Robots* published? _____
9. Which book was published in Chicago? _____
10. Who is the author of the book about robots? _____

**At Home:** Think about a subject that interests you. Then make up the information for a book on this subject and write a subject card for it.

**49**

**McGraw-Hill Language Arts
Grade 4, Unit 3, Study Skills,
pages 206–207**  **10**

# Vocabulary: Prefixes

- A **prefix** is a word part added to the beginning of a word. A prefix changes the meaning of the base word.

- A **base word** is a word to which a prefix is added.
  **in + complete     dis + obey     im + perfect**

- You can figure out the meaning of a word by putting together the meaning of the prefix with the meaning of the base word.

| Prefix | Meaning |
|--------|---------|
| dis | not, opposite of |
| im | not, without |
| in | not without |
| mis | wrongly or opposite of |
| non | not |
| re | again |

Choose a word from the word box that completes each sentence. Write it on the line. Then circle the prefix of the word you write.

| | | | | |
|---|---|---|---|---|
| uncomfortable | multiscreen | impossible | dislike | previews |
| impatient | unreal | recount | misunderstand | disbelief |

**1.** I go to movies at a _____ theater.

**2.** I like to watch movie _____.

**3.** Sometimes I am _____ with the action.

**4.** That's when I _____ the story to my friends.

**5.** Some movies make me feel _____.

**6.** I _____ lots of gooey romantic stuff.

**7.** Special effects can show things that are _____.

**8.** My sister doesn't like movies that are _____.

**9.** I just listen to her in _____.

**10.** Maybe I just _____ her.

**At Home:** In a dictionary, look up each prefix you circled and write its definition.

# Composition Skills: Leads and Endings

- The first sentence in a persuasive composition is the **lead.** It should capture the attention of your reader.

    *I remember when I first met Max.*

- The last sentence is the **ending.** To help your reader feel that your writing is complete, end by drawing a conclusion, summarizing the main idea, or restating it.

    *Now I believe in happy endings.*

Circle the word *lead* or *ending* for each sentence.

1. The book sale you've been waiting for will take place next week.

    lead          ending

2. So, I ask for your vote as student representative for our class.

    lead          ending

3. You'll never regret hiring Darla as your pet sitter.

    lead          ending

4. Why do students want to be volunteers?

    lead          ending

5. Never forget that recycling protects the environment.

    lead          ending

6. Would you like to run faster and feel healthier?

    lead          ending

7. Some students in our school will start a math tutoring service.

    lead          ending

8. Now you know that bicycle riders with helmets are also smart riders.

    lead          ending

9. Have you signed up for an after-school activity yet?

    lead          ending

10. Talented students are available as tutors in a new student tutoring program.

    lead          ending

**At Home:** Pick a lead or ending that you like from the exercise above. For a lead, write an appropriate ending. For an ending, write an appropriate lead.

51

**McGraw-Hill Language Arts**
Grade 4, Unit 3 Composition Skills,
pages 212–213

10

McGraw-Hill School Division

# Adjectives

┌─ **RULES** ─────────────────────────────────────────────┐

**Adjectives**  } are words that describe nouns.
can tell **what kind** and **how many.**
usually come before the nouns they describe.

*Elephants are **large** animals.*    *There are **two** kinds of elephants.*

*There are **African** elephants.*    *There are **Indian** elephants.*

└────────────────────────────────────────────────────────┘

Circle the adjective in each sentence. Write the noun that the adjective describes.

1. Elephants are strong animals. _____

2. They are also intelligent animals. _____

3. The trunk of an elephant is a remarkable feature. _____

4. It can be used for many purposes. _____

5. The trunk can be used to drink or spray cool water. _____

6. It can be used to pick up a small nut. _____

7. It can also be used to rip up a huge tree. _____

8. Elephants can be trained to be excellent helpers. _____

9. They can easily move heavy objects. _____

10. They can carry people on their strong backs. _____

11. Elephants live together in large groups. _____

12. They can live for many years. _____

13. People used to hunt elephants for ivory tusks. _____

14. The beautiful tusks were used to make things. _____

15. Today, strict laws protect elephants from hunters. _____

┌──┐
│15│ **McGraw-Hill Language Arts**
└──┘ **Grade 4, Unit 4, Adjectives,**
     **pages 262–263**

**At Home:** Write a description about something or someone. Include as many adjectives as you can.

52

# Articles: *a, an, the*

┌─ **RULES** ─────────────────────────────────────────────┐

The words *a, an,* and *the* are special adjectives called **articles**.

- Use *a* and *an* before singular nouns. Use *a* if the next word begins with a consonant sound. Use *an* if the next word begins with a vowel sound.

    *A lynx is **an** animal.*

- Use *the* before a singular noun that names a particular person, place, or thing.

    *The lynx is a kind of wild cat.*

- Use *the* before plural nouns.

    *The mountains are home to some wildcats.*

└──────────────────────────────────────────────────────────┘

Choose the correct article in parentheses to complete each sentence. Write it on the line.

1. _____ elephant may use its trunk to pet her baby. (A, An)

2. _____ ostrich uses its long, powerful toes for defense. (The, A)

3. Stripes on _____ zebra help it hide from its enemies. (a, an)

4. _____ anteater really eats ants. (A, An)

5. At birth, _____ giraffe is about six feet tall. (a, an)

6. Cheetahs are _____ animals that can run the fastest. (an, the)

7. The tongue of _____ chameleon is as long as its body. (a, an)

8. _____ bee hummingbird is the smallest of all birds. (An, The)

9. _____ coconut crab can climb trees. (A, An)

10. _____ eagle's eyes are made so that it can see from great distances. (A, An)

**At Home:** Write five adjectives about your favorite animal. Include at least one article in each sentence.

**McGraw-Hill Language Arts Grade 4, Unit 4, Adjectives, pages 264–265**

53

10

McGraw-Hill School Division

# Adjectives After Linking Verbs

**RULES**

- An **adjective** is a word that describes a noun.
- Sometimes an adjective **follows** the noun it describes.
- When an adjective follows the noun it describes, the noun and adjective are connected by a **linking verb.**
- The **linking verb** is usually a form of the verb *be.*

  Summer *is* wonderful.          The days *are* long.
  The temperature *was* high.          The days *were* sunny.

Circle each linking verb. Then write the adjective that describes each underlined noun.

1. The <u>summer</u> is relaxing. _____

2. The long <u>days</u> are warm. _____

3. <u>Sports</u> in the summer are fun. _____

4. <u>Swimming</u> in the lake is popular. _____

5. Last <u>summer</u> was perfect for me. _____

6. Winter <u>days</u> are shorter. _____

7. Winter <u>weather</u> is colder. _____

8. Last <u>winter</u> was snowy. _____

9. Many <u>days</u> were freezing. _____

10. Sometimes winter <u>days</u> are beautiful. _____

# Mechanics and Usage: Proper Adjectives

> **RULES**
>
> - **Proper adjectives** are formed from proper nouns. They refer to a particular person, place, or thing.
> - **Proper adjectives** are always capitalized.
>
> | | | |
> |---|---|---|
> | *Europe* ⟶ | *European* | *European* explorers |
> | *North America* ⟶ | *North American* | *North American* coast |

Underline each proper adjective. Then write the noun it describes.

1. Have you read about American history? _____

2. Christopher Columbus was an Italian citizen. _____

3. He sailed to America for a Spanish queen. _____

4. Columbus landed on a Caribbean island. _____

5. He never landed on the North American mainland. _____

6. A German mapmaker named the Americas. _____

7. Spanish explorers arrived in Mexico. _____

8. A Portuguese sailor landed in South America. _____

9. Many Italian explorers traveled to America. _____

10. John Cabot made the first English voyage
    to North America. _____

11. Jamestown was the first British settlement
    in North America. _____

12. Many Spanish missions were built in the west. _____

13. The new world also saw the arrival of French
    traders. _____

14. The early colonies were ruled by an English king. _____

15. People from other European countries also
    settled here. _____

**At Home:** List the names of five countries you have heard of. Then write a sentence about each one. Include a proper adjective in each sentence.

55

**McGraw-Hill Language Arts**
**Grade 4, Unit 4, Adjectives,**
**pages 268–269**

/15

McGraw-Hill School Division

# Mixed Review

> **RULES**
>
> • An **adjective** is a word that describes a noun. Adjectives tell *what kind* and *how many*.   **red** flower   **old** house   **two** teams
>
> • When an adjective comes after a noun it describes, the two are connected by a **linking verb.**
>
>   Summer **is** wonderful.   The temperatures **are** warm.
>
> • **Proper** adjectives are formed from proper nouns. A **proper adjective** is always capitalized.   Europe → European   **European** countries

**A.** Underline each adjective. Then write the noun it describes.

1. People have interesting hobbies. _____

2. I knew someone that collected ancient coins. _____

3. The coins are valuable because of their age. _____

4. My grandfather makes ship models. _____

5. He keeps the models in display cases. _____

6. He has at least seven models on display. _____

7. My grandmother collects and dries wild flowers. _____

8. She arranges them in glass vases. _____

9. I like to make miniature models. _____

10. I have twelve airplanes hanging in my room. _____

**B.** Write each proper adjective correctly. Circle the noun it describes.

11. I saw a collection of native american pottery. _____

12. There is a collection of asian art at the museum. _____

13. I have a book about the egyptian pyramids. _____

14. My brother wrote an article about mexican carvings. _____

15. The museum has some examples of roman sculpture. _____

**McGraw-Hill Language Arts**
**Grade 4, Unit 4, Mixed Review,**
**pages 270–271**

15

**At Home:** Do you or a member of your family collect something? Write a paragraph about the collection. Then underline each adjective you used and circle the noun it describes.

56

# Adjectives That Compare

## RULES

- Adjectives that compare nouns often end in **-er** or **-est.**
- An adjective + **-er** compares two people, places, or things.
  *Cats are **faster** than dogs.*
- An adjective + **-est** compares more than two people, places, or things.
  *Cheetahs are the **fastest** animals.*

Write the correct form of the adjective in parentheses.

1. Cats are usually (smaller, smallest) than dogs. _____

2. Cats are among the (cleaner, cleanest) animals of all. _____

3. Cats have (sharper, sharpest) vision than humans. _____

4. Cats have (sharper, sharpest) claws than dogs. _____

5. Some cats are (quicker, quickest) eaters than others. _____

6. Persian cats have the (longer, longest) hair of all cats. _____

7. Rex cats have the (shorter, shortest) hair of any cat. _____

8. Persian cats have (fuller, fullest) tails than Burmese cats. _____

9. Siamese cats are among the (louder, loudest) cats. _____

10. Angora cats are one of the (older, oldest) kinds of all cats. _____

Maine Coon    Manx    Siamese    Persian

**At Home:** Make a list of adjectives that compare. Try to use at least one of the adjectives each day until you have used them all.

57

**McGraw-Hill Language Arts**
**Grade 4, Unit 4, Adjectives,**
**pages 272–273**

10

McGraw-Hill School Division

# Spelling Adjectives That Compare

```
┌─ RULES ═══════════════════════════════════════════════════════════════╗
When adding -er or -est to adjectives, follow these spelling rules:
• If an adjective ends with e, drop the e, then add -er or -est.
    little (drop the e): littler   littlest
• If an adjective ends with a consonant and a y, change the y to i and
  add -er or -est.
    heavy (change y to i): heavier   heaviest
• If an adjective has a single vowel before a final consonant, double the
  final consonant, then add -er or -est.
    flat (double final consonant): flatter   flattest
╚═══════════════════════════════════════════════════════════════════════╝
```

Write the correct -er or -est form of the adjective in parentheses ( ).

**1.** (hot) This summer is _____ than last summer.

**2.** (nice) My flower garden is _____ than last year's garden.

**3.** (pretty) The roses are _____ this year than last year.

**4.** (lovely) I think red roses are the _____ of all the roses.

**5.** (large) My neighbor's vegetable garden is _____ than mine.

**6.** (tasty) My tomatoes are _____ than my neighbor's tomatoes.

**7.** (tiny) Cherry tomatoes are _____ than plum tomatoes.

**8.** (heavy) I grew the _____ squash in the neighborhood.

**9.** (huge) My uncle grew the _____ pumpkin I ever saw.

**10.** (happy) Gardeners are the _____ people you'll ever meet.

**McGraw-Hill Language Arts**
**Grade 4, Unit 4, Adjectives,**
**pages 274–275**

**At Home:** Write five sentences about something you like to
do. Include at least one adjective that changes its spelling
in each sentence.

58

McGraw-Hill School Division

10

# Comparing with *More* and *Most*

---

**RULES**

- Use **more** or **most** with most longer adjectives. Use *more* to compare two people places or things. Use *most* to compare more than two people, places, or things.

    *I think plays are **more enjoyable** than movies.*

    *I think plays are the **most enjoyable** form of entertainment.*

- Never use **more** or **most** with an adjective that already has an **-er** or **-est** ending.

---

Choose the word in parentheses that completes each sentence.

1. Our local theater is (more, most) impressive
   this year than last year.                          _____

2. This year's play is the (more, most) entertaining
   one we have put on.                                _____

3. The costumes are the (more, most) beautiful
   I have ever seen.                                  _____

4. The stage sets are (more, most) elaborate
   than they were last year.                          _____

5. The actors are the (more, most) effective
   performers in this state.                          _____

6. Last night's performance was (more, most)
   enjoyable than yesterday's performance.            _____

7. The performers seemed (more, most) relaxed
   than they were yesterday.                          _____

8. The leading character is the (more, most)
   interesting part of all.                           _____

9. The actress who plays the part is the (more, most)
   popular of all the performers.                     _____

10. She is the (more, most) prepared of anyone
    in the show.                                      _____

---

**At Home:** Think of two television programs you like to watch. Write five sentences comparing them using *more* or *most*.

McGraw-Hill School Division

# Comparing with *Good* and *Bad*

┌─ **RULES** ──────────────────────────────────────────────┐

• The adjectives *good* and *bad* have special forms when used to compare.

• Use **better** and **worse** to compare two people, places, or things.

   *This summer was **better** than last summer.*
   *Last summer was **worse** than this summer.*

• Use **best** or **worst** to compare more than two people, places, or things.

   *This was the **best** summer I can remember.*
   *Last summer was the **worst** summer I can remember.*

└──────────────────────────────────────────────────────────┘

Write the correct form of the word in parentheses ( ) to complete each sentence.

1. This summer camp was _____ than the last one. (good)

2. The lake was the _____ I ever swam in. (good)

3. My swimming team was _____ than my friend's team. (bad)

4. The camp counselors were the _____ I've ever had. (good)

5. The food was the _____ I ever tasted. (bad)

6. The crafts classes were _____ than the woodworking classes. (good)

7. The soccer coaches were _____ than the baseball coaches. (bad)

8. Swimming was _____ than hiking. (good)

9. The camp singing was the _____ I ever heard. (bad)

10. Hiking was _____ than bird watching. (good)

**McGraw-Hill Language Arts**
Grade 4, Unit 4, Adjectives,
`10` pages 278–279

**At Home:** Write five sentences comparing two summers you can remember. Use forms of good or bad in each sentence.

**60**

# Combining Sentences: Adjectives

**RULES**

You can sometimes combine sentences by writing the adjective from one sentence in the other. Leave out the words that are the same in both sentences.

> ***Rico saw some monkeys.*** *The monkeys were* ***playful.***
>
> ***Rico saw some playful monkeys.***

Write each pair of sentences as one sentence.

1. Rico visited a zoo. The zoo was interesting.

   _____

2. He saw some lions. The lions were scary.

   _____

3. He watched some elephants. The elephants were enormous.

   _____

4. Rico watched the elephants being fed. The elephants were hungry.

   _____

5. After they ate, the elephants did some tricks. The tricks were clever.

   _____

6. Rico visited the reptile exhibit. The exhibit was new.

   _____

7. There were many kinds of snakes. The snakes were exotic.

   _____

8. There were also many lizards. The lizards were unusual.

   _____

9. Then Rico went to see the birds. The birds were tropical.

   _____

10. There were many kinds of parrots. The parrots were colorful.

   _____

**At Home:** Write three pairs of sentences about a place you have visited. Then combine each pair into one sentence.

**McGraw-Hill Language Arts**
**Grade 4, Unit 4, Adjectives,**
**pages 280–281**

61

10

McGraw-Hill School Division

# Mechanics and Usage: Letter Punctuation

---

**┌─ RULES ═══════════════════════════════**

- The greeting and closing of a letter should begin with capital letters.
- Use a comma after the greeting and the closing of a friendly letter.
- Use a comma between the names of a city and a state.
- Use a comma between the day and the year in a date.

                                    237 Bridge Road
                                    Bangor, Maine ←**city and state**
                                    July 28, 2001  ←**day and year**

**greeting**→ **D**ear Maria**,**

          I just came back from vacation. My family
          and I went to Yellowstone National Park.
          I will tell you all about it when you visit.

                              **Y**our friend**,** ←**closing**
                              Alana

---

Write each letter part. Add the correct punctuation mark or capital letter.

**1.** dear Uncle Joe,          _____

**2.** Madison Wisconsin        _____

**3.** sincerely yours,         _____

**4.** dear friend              _____

**5.** May 7 2001               _____

**6.** chicago illinois         _____

**7.** your pal                 _____

**8.** june 6 2001              _____

**9.** dear mom                 _____

**10.** your friend             _____

**McGraw-Hill Language Arts**
**Grade 4, Unit 4, Adjectives,**
**pages 282–283**
10

**At Home:** Write a letter to a friend. Check to see if you
punctuated and capitalized correctly

62

# Mixed Review

- An adjective can compare two people, places, or things:

| | |
|---|---|
| **adjective** + **-er** | *Soccer is a **faster** game than tennis.* |
| **more** + **adjective** | *I think soccer is **more exciting** than basketball.* |
| **better** or **worse** | *I play soccer **better** than baseball.* |

- An adjective can compare more than two people, places, or things:

| | |
|---|---|
| **adjective** + **-est** | *We had the **fastest** team ever.* |
| **most** + **adjective** | *Baseball is the **most popular** sport of all.* |
| **best** or **worst** | *We had the **best** game of the season.* |

- **Combine sentences** that tell about the same person, place, or thing.

  *Soccer is a game.     Soccer is fast.*
  *Soccer is a fast game.*

**A.** Write the correct form of the word or words in parentheses ( ).

1. Juan is (better, best) at soccer than I am.                    _____

2. Hector is the (stronger, strongest) player of all.         _____

3. Megan is a (faster, fastest) runner than Tony.            _____

4. Yoshi had the (higher, highest) score on the team.      _____

5. This was my (worse, worst) year ever at baseball.       _____

**B.** Write each pair of sentences as one sentence.

6. The soccer game was about to begin. It was the last soccer game.

   _____

7. We watched the soccer game. The soccer game was exciting.

   _____

8. We cheered for our team. Our team was winning.

   _____

9. Our team scored a point. It was the winning point.

   _____

10. The fans cheered the team. The team was victorious.

    _____

**At Home:** Write about a sport that you or some member of your family enjoys. Circle the adjectives that compare.

**McGraw-Hill Language Arts**
**Grade 4, Unit 4, Mixed Review,**
**pages 284–285**

63                                                                                          10

McGraw-Hill School Division

# Common Errors: Adjectives

┌─ **RULES** ─────────────────────────────────────────┐

- short adjective + **-er** compares two people, places, or things

    *Trees are **larger** than bushes.*

- **more** + long adjective compares two people, places, or things

    *Flowers are **more colorful** than leaves.*

- adjective + **-est** compare more than two people, places, or things

    *Trees are the **largest** plants.*

- **most** + long adjective compare more than two people, places, or things

    *I think orchids are the **most colorful** flowers.*

- Never use **more** or **most** with an adjective that already ends in **-er** or **-est.**

    *Wrong: Trees are **more larger** than bushes.*
    *Wrong: Trees are the **most largest** of all plants.*

└─────────────────────────────────────────────────────┘

Write the correct form of the adjective in parentheses ( ) on the line.

1. Bristlecone pine trees are the (old) living things on earth. _____

2. Giant sequoia trees are the (large) living things. _____

3. Coconut seeds are the (big) of all seeds. _____

4. A cactus environment is (dry) than a woodland forest. _____

5. A tropical rain forest is (wet) than a grassland. _____

6. Roses are the (beautiful) of all flowers. _____

7. Some orchids are the (rare) of all plants. _____

8. A tree is (tall) than a shrub. _____

9. A baobob tree is (unusual) than an oak tree. _____

10. A fern is (delicate) than a cactus. _____

McGraw-Hill School Division

10 **McGraw-Hill Language Arts**
**Grade 4, Unit 4, Adjectives,**
**pages 286–287**

**At Home:** Look around your house or neighborhood for plants. Write sentences that compare them. Use the correct forms of the adjectives that compare.

64

# Study Skills: Maps

There are many kinds of maps.

- A **political map** shows how land is divided into states or countries.
- A **physical map** shows mountains, plains, deserts, bodies of water, and valleys.
- A **road map** shows roads in an area.

To understand a map, you can use the following:

- a **compass rose** to point out the directions north, south, east, and west.
- a **legend** or **key** to show the meanings of the symbols on the map.
- a **scale** to show how far it is from one place to another.

Study the map and then answer the questions below.

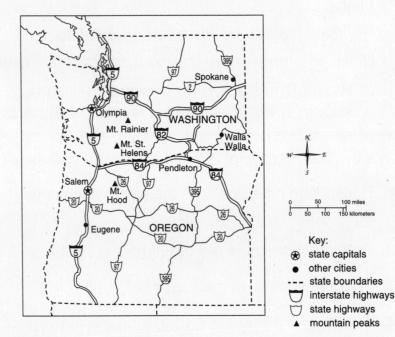

1. What direction would you travel if you were going from Eugene, Oregon, to Olympia, Washington?

   _____

2. What are three mountain peaks on this map?

   _____

3. About how far in miles is it from Spokane, Washington, to Pendleton,

   Oregon? _____

4. About how far in kilometers is it from Pendleton, Oregon, to Walla Walla,

   Washington? _____

5. What is the capital of Oregon? _____

**At Home:** Plan a trip from Eugene, Oregon, to Spokane, Washington. Write out a set of traveling directions and describe what you might see along the way.

**McGraw-Hill Language Arts
Grade 4, Unit 4, Study Skills,
pages 294–295**    5

McGraw-Hill School Division

# Vocabulary: Synonyms and Antonyms

- A **synonym** is a word that means the same or almost the same as another word.
  sad/gloomy    huge/enormous    pleasant/nice
- An **antonym** is a word that means the opposite of another word.
  happy/sad    big/small    right/wrong

After each pair of words, write **A** for antonyms or **S** for synonyms.

1. gigantic/enormous _____
2. fiction/nonfiction _____
3. messy/neat _____
4. baby/infant _____
5. old/aged _____
6. confused/muddled _____
7. narrow/wide _____
8. yell/shout _____
9. small/tiny _____
10. possess/own _____
11. moist/dry _____
12. angry/mad _____
13. fake/real _____
14. shiny/dull _____
15. stop/start _____
16. high/low _____
17. breezy/windy _____
18. opened/closed _____
19. slowly/quickly _____
20. quickly/speedily _____

**McGraw-Hill Language Arts**
Grade 4, Unit 4, Vocabulary,
pages 296–297

20

**At Home:** Write three pairs of synonyms and three pairs of antonyms. Use them in sentences.

66

McGraw-Hill School Division

# Composition: Organization

- Certain words and phrases can help you organize your ideas logically.
- Words like *inside, outside, over, beside, above, near, next to,* and *on top of* are **spatial words.** Spatial words tell where things are found or arranged.
- Words like *first, next, then, later, after that, as soon as,* and *a long time ago* are **time-order words.** They show when things happen and in what order.

  **Spatial order:** *Is the book <u>beside</u> the lamp or <u>next</u> to the CD player?*
  **Time order:** *<u>As soon as</u> your name is called, walk up to the stage.*

Underline spatial or time-order words used in each sentence. Then, circle **spatial** or **time-order** to identify the kind of words.

1. There's an eagle's nest on top of the cliff.     spatial     time-order

2. Which did you see first, the mole or the snake?     spatial     time-order

3. The mother alligator appeared, then a baby alligator followed.     spatial     time-order

4. Was it a long time ago that the cat had kittens?     spatial     time-order

5. An adult bird stands above the babies and feeds them worms.     spatial     time-order

6. Our canoe slid over the rocks and white water.     spatial     time-order

7. The horses happily graze near the barn.     spatial     time-order

8. Don't wait until later to feed the hungry chicks.     spatial     time-order

9. Is the corral behind the house or the barn?     spatial     time-order

10. After a long walk, we rested.     spatial     time-order

**At Home:** Write two sentences about your notebook. Organize one sentence with spatial words and the other with time-order words.

67

McGraw-Hill School Division

**McGraw-Hill Language Arts** Grade 4, Unit 4, Composition Skills, pages 296–297     10

# Pronouns

┌─ **RULES** ─────────────────────────────────────────┐

- A **pronoun** is a word that replaces one or more nouns.

- A **pronoun** must agree with the noun it replaces.

 *That **boy** asked if **he** could dress up like a soldier.*

 **singular noun singular pronoun**

 *The **soldiers** did not realize **they** had no place to retreat.*

 **plural noun          plural pronoun**

└────────────────────────────────────────────────────┘

Underline the pronoun in each sentence. Then write each noun that the pronoun replaces.

1. Mrs. Harris said she will teach about the Civil War. _____

2. The Battle of Antietam is remembered because it was an important battle of the Civil War. _____

3. We talked about the generals and how they set out to win. _____

4. General Robert E. Lee's soldiers didn't know they were in a bad position.

 _____

5. The Union General George McClellan thought he would drive Lee's soldiers into the Potomac. _____

6. General Stonewell Jackson's men must have been shocked when they were attacked by Union soldiers. _____

7. Jackson's lines were badly hurt and they were forced to retreat. _____

8. The Confederates fled to the fields as they retreated from Union soldiers. _____

9. Union soldiers were unaware of what they would soon be facing. _____

Lee      McClellan     Jackson

10. Some historians consider the Battle of Antietam a Union victory although over two thousand soldiers died in it. _____

# Subject Pronouns

┌─ **RULES** ─────────────────────────────────────────┐

- A **subject pronoun** is a pronoun that can be used as the subject of a sentence.

  **Singular:** *I, you, he, she, it*

      *I want to be a geologist.*

  **Plural:**   *we, you, they*

      ***They** try to predict earthquakes and volcanic eruptions.*

└─────────────────────────────────────────────────────┘

Write a pronoun to replace the underlined subject part of each sentence.

1. <u>Dr. David Massaro</u> planned a unit about volcanoes for his science class.

              _____

2. <u>Our class</u> just finished learning about earthquakes. _____

3. <u>A volcano</u> is a destructive natural force. _____

4. <u>The students in my class</u> learned that most volcanoes occur

in an area called the Ring of Fire. _____

5. <u>The volcanic eruptions</u> occur as a result of plate movements

within the earth. _____

6. <u>A volcano</u> releases hot poisonous gases into the air. _____

7. <u>Some eruptions</u> form volcanic islands. _____

8. <u>These mountain islands</u> build up from the ocean floor. _____

9. <u>Valerie</u> wanted to know how far volcanic debris can travel. _____

10. <u>The teacher</u> explained that erupting debris can travel for miles. _____

11. <u>The lava from a volcano</u> can affect towns located miles away. _____

12. <u>Mount St. Helens</u> violently erupted in 1980. _____

13. <u>Many Washington citizens</u> were not prepared for this eruption. _____

14. <u>The ashes</u> covered a huge area. _____

15. <u>Scientists</u> are trying to predict when volcanoes will erupt. _____

McGraw-Hill School Division

---

**At Home:** Rewrite the above sentences using the correct subject pronoun in place of the underlined words.

**McGraw-Hill Language Arts**
**Grade 4, Unit 5, Pronouns,**
**pages 346–347**

/15

# Object Pronouns

**RULES**

- **Object pronouns** generally appear in the predicate of a sentence.

  **Singular:** *me, you, him, her, it*

  **Plural:** *us, you, them*

- **Object pronouns** may be used after an action verb or after a word such as *for, at, of, with,* or *to.*

  *The teacher <u>made</u> **our class** write a report. The teacher <u>made</u> **us** write a report.*

  *Students cooperated <u>with</u> **the teacher**. Students cooperated <u>with</u> **her**.*

Underline the object pronoun in each sentence and write it on the line.

1. You warned me this class would be hard. _____

2. I told you to plan wisely. _____

3. Mrs. McMadden gave them work to do. _____

4. They didn't expect her to assign a project so soon. _____

5. She had a report for me to write. _____

6. The teacher chose the topics for us. _____

7. Students wondered what topic she would give them. _____

8. Jimmy said he would ask her for an easy subject. _____

9. Mrs. McMadden said she was not happy with him. _____

10. He looked at her with a confused expression. _____

11. She wanted him to change his attitude. _____

12. After the teacher gave the topics to them, they were relieved. _____

13. Each of us had the same topic. _____

14. They thought that was very kind of her. _____

15. Now I can work with you on the project. _____

**At Home:** Make up sentences using the object pronouns
*me, us, you, him, her,* or *them.* Say your sentences aloud
to a family member.

McGraw-Hill School Division

# Mechanics and Usage: Punctuation in Dialogue

┌─ **RULES** ─────────────────────────────────────────┐

**Dialogue** is the exact words spoken by the characters in a story.

• Always use quotation marks at the beginning and end of dialogue.

   *Mother said, "Let's plan a vacation!"*

• Begin a speaker's words with a capital letter.

   *"**We** can go camping," Dad suggested.*

• Begin a new paragraph whenever a new person speaks.

   *"The National Parks are always fun. Maybe we'll even see a bear at our campsite!" Jamie exclaimed.*

   *"I'd rather stay in a hotel," Sean whined.*

└─────────────────────────────────────────────────────┘

Write the letter *C* before the dialogue that is written correctly.

1. _____    Dad said, "Camping would save us some money."

   _____    "Dad said, camping would save us some money."

2. _____    "Gee, Dad. We've been saving for this trip all year," Mom said.

   _____    Gee, Dad. "We've been saving for this trip all year." Mom said.

3. _____    Well, how about a compromise? "He suggested."

   _____    "Well, how about a compromise?" he suggested.

4. _____    "We could stay in a hotel on our way to one of the National Parks. Does that sound like a good idea?" Dad asked.

   _____    "We could stay in a hotel on our way to one of the National Parks. "Does that sound like a good idea?" Dad asked.

5. _____    Mom replied, Let's hear what our children have to say about it."
              "I'll go along with it, as long as I get to camp out!" said Sean.

   _____    Mom replied, "Let's hear what the children have to say about it."
              "I'll go along with it, as long as I get to camp out!" said Sean.

**At Home:** Ask your family to plan a trip. Write down a few sentences of your family's dialogue.

71

**McGraw-Hill Language Arts**
**Grade 4, Unit 5, Pronouns,**
**pages 350–351**   5

McGraw-Hill School Division

# Mixed Review

**RULES**

- A **subject pronoun** is used as the subject of a sentence.

    **Singular:** *I, you, he, she, it* → *She* wants to go to New York City.

    **Plural:** *we, you, they* → *We* were planning our summer vacation.

- An **object pronoun** is used after an action verb or a word such as *in, into, to, with, for, by,* or *at.*

    **Singular:** *me, you, him, her, it* → They asked *me* where I wanted to go.

    **Plural:** *us, you, them* → Who is going to go with *us*?

- Use **quotation marks** before and after a person's exact words.

    *"I would like to go someplace unusual,"* I said.

Rewrite each sentence. Replace each underlined noun with the correct pronoun. Add quotation marks and capital letters where needed.

1. <u>Mom</u> said, let's go to the Statue of Liberty.

   _____

2. <u>the Statue of Liberty</u> is in New York City, she told us.

   _____

3. it was given to the united states by france, <u>Dad</u> explained.

   _____

4. <u>your mother and i</u> saw it many years ago, he said.

   _____

5. this summer might be a good time for <u>the family</u> to go, Dad suggested.

   _____

**McGraw-Hill Language Arts**
**Grade 4, Unit 5, Mixed Review,**
**pages 352–353**

**5**

**At Home:** Think of some place you have visited with your family. Make up a conversation about it with one of your family members. Use some subject and object pronouns in your conversation. Punctuate correctly.

72

# Pronoun-Verb Agreement

┌─ **RULES** ─────────────────────────────────────────────┐

- Add **-s** or **-es** to most action verbs in the present tense when using the pronouns *he*, *she*, or *it*.

  *He* **wins** *the prize.*      *She* **watches** *happily.*

- When using the pronouns *I*, *we*, *you*, or *they*, do not add **-s** or **-es** to a present tense action verb.

  *You* **ride** *the bike.*      *I* **watch** *the race.*

└─────────────────────────────────────────────────────────┘

Circle the correct verb in parentheses that agrees with the subject pronoun.

1. He (plan, plans) to run in the triathlon this weekend.

2. She (train, trains) for the race also.

3. We (hope, hopes) one of them will be able to win.

4. At first, they (swim, swims) in the lake for 1.5 miles.

5. Then they (ride, rides) their bikes from the park to the center of town.

6. Finally, it (end, ends) with a three-mile run through the streets downtown.

7. We (hope, hopes) to watch the entire race.

8. They (start, starts) the competition at 7:00 A.M. sharp.

9. It (take, takes) over an hour to complete the course.

10. She (race, races) toward the finish line.

**At Home:** Write a paragraph about a time you were in some kind of competition. Use subject pronouns in your account.

73

**McGraw-Hill Language Arts**
**Grade 4, Unit 5, Pronouns,**
**pages 354–355**     10

# Combining Sentences

┌─ **RULES** ──────────────────────────────────────────┐
- You can **combine sentences** that have similar ideas by joining **pronouns** in either the subject or the predicate.

  She planned a class party. I planned a class party.
  ***She*** and ***I*** *planned a class party.*
└──────────────────────────────────────────────────────┘

Combine each pair of sentences. Use *and* or *or.*

**1.** She will make the decorations. I will make the decorations.

_____

**2.** Does the scissors belong to you? Does the scissors belong to them?

_____

**3.** You want to help plan the menu. I want to help plan the menu.

_____

**4.** You should call the class officers. I should call the class officers.

_____

**5.** Did he return our phone calls? Did she return our phone calls?

_____

**6.** You can invite former teachers. I can invite former teachers.

_____

**7.** I might not recognize him. I might not recognize her.

_____

**8.** Tim will give a balloon to you. Tim will give a balloon to me.

_____

**9.** He will be glad to see you. He will be glad to see me.

_____

**10.** Will he be able to attend? Will she be able to attend?

_____

# Possessive Pronouns

## RULES

- A **possessive pronoun** is a pronoun that shows ownership by one or more persons, places, or things.

| | | | | | |
|---|---|---|---|---|---|
| *my* | *your* | *his* | *her* | *its* | *our* |
| *their* | *mine* | *ours* | *hers* | *yours* | *theirs* |

- Some possessive pronouns can be used alone.

    *These are **Keri's** fossils.*     *These are **hers.***

Choose a possessive pronoun from the box above that means the same as the words in parentheses.

1. Is this ____ book about fossils? (belonging to you)  _____

2. Who is ____ author? (belonging to it)  _____

3. Gina Larocca is ____ name. (belonging to a female)  _____

4. Collecting fossils is a favorite hobby of ____.

   (belonging to me)  _____

5. One of ____ teachers in the fourth grade has a

   display of mold and cast fossils. (belonging to us)  _____

6. She will show us how to make mold fossils like ____.

   (belonging to her)  _____

7. Her mold fossils were made when animals left ____

   footprints in a patch of muddy soil. (belonging to them)  _____

8. ____ will be made by making imprints of leaves on

   soft clay. (belonging to us)  _____

9. The other science classes will be making hand imprints

   in plaster to create ____. (belonging to them)  _____

10. George will try to make a cast fossil from the imprint

    of ____ hand by using it as a mold. (belonging to him)  _____

**At Home:** Choose five possessive pronouns from the box above. Make up a sentence for each. Say the sentences aloud to a parent or sister or brother.

**McGraw-Hill Language Arts**
**Grade 4, Unit 5, Pronouns,**
**pages 358–359**

10

McGraw-Hill School Division

# Mechanics and Usage: Contractions—Pronouns and Verbs

┌─ **RULES** ─────────────────────────────────────────────┐

• A pronoun and a verb can be combined to form a **contraction.**

   *She is* **She's**          *You are* **You're**          *We have* **We've**

• The contractions **it's, you're,** and **they're** should not be confused with the possessive pronouns **its, your,** and **their.**

   ***It's*** *time to give your dog **its** bath.*
   ***You're*** *going to need to bring **your** supply of towels.*
   *You will find that **they're** in **their** proper place on the shelf.*

└─────────────────────────────────────────────────────────┘

Underline the word in parentheses that correctly completes the sentence.

1. (Your, You're) lucky that you were not born in the early 1800s.

2. (It's, Its) the time when Americans were trying to extend the frontier.

3. (You've, You're) probably heard about the hard life of the pioneers.

4. (They're, They'd) travel westward by wagon trains.

5. (Its, It's) hard to imagine traveling by wagon train across the Great Plains.

6. The American frontier has many heroes in (its, it's) history.

7. (We're, We've) all heard of Daniel Boone and Davy Crockett.

8. (They're, Their) two of the most famous frontiersmen.

9. Boone explored Kentucky for the pioneers and blazed (they're, their) trails.

10. (His, He's) known as a generous leader who led westward-moving settlers

    through a route called The Wilderness Road.

11. (It's, Its) a route through rugged parts of the Appalachian Mountains.

12. (You're, Your) teacher may have told you about Davy Crockett.

13. (We've, We're) come to associate Davy Crockett's name with the Alamo.

14. These famous frontiersmen tamed the wilderness through (their, they're) hard work.

15. (Your, You're) library's encyclopedia has more information about them.

# Mixed Review

┌─ **RULES** ─────────────────────────────────────────────────

• **Present tense verbs** must agree with their **subject pronouns.**

  **Singular Subject Pronouns:** *I, you, he, she, it*   *He travels on weekends.*

  **Plural Subject Pronouns:**   *we, you, they*        *They travel on weekends.*

• A **possessive pronoun** takes the place of one or more possessive nouns.

  *Cindy's piano teacher was very good. Her piano teacher was very good.*

  **Singular Possessive Pronouns:** *my, yours, his, her, its*

  **Plural Possessive Pronouns:**   *our, your, their*

• A **contraction** is a shortened form of two words, such as a pronoun and a verb. An apostrophe (') shows the missing letters.

  *I'm = I am      we're = we are      they'll = they will*

• Don't confuse the contractions *it's, they're,* and *you're* with the possessive pronouns *its, their,* and *your.*

└──────────────────────────────────────────────────────────

Rewrite each sentence. Form contractions from the underlined pronouns and verbs. Substitute possessive pronouns for underlined possessive nouns.

1. It is going to be fun at Mike's party this weekend.

   _____

2. We are going to see my brother's Little League game.

   _____

3. They have bought tickets for my sister's talent show.

   _____

4. She is going to see Betty's new house.

   _____

5. We have some time before John's piano recital begins.

   _____

**At Home:** Write five sentences about things your family likes to do on weekends. Include some possessive pronouns and contractions. **77** Be sure the verbs and subjects in your sentences agree.

**McGraw-Hill Language Arts Grade 4, Unit 5, Mixed Review, pages 362–363** 5

McGraw-Hill School Division

## Common Errors: Pronouns

```
┌─ RULES ────────────────────────────────────────────────────────┐

  • Use a **subject pronoun** as the        • Use an **object pronoun** after an
    subject of a sentence.                     action verb or after words such as
                                               *for, at, of, with, in, to,* or *by.*

  **Singular:** *I, you, he, she, it*         **Singular:** *me, you, him, her, it*
  **Plural:** *we, you, they*                 **Plural:** *us, you, them*

  *I always wanted to learn how to swim.*   *I found a course just right for **me**.*

  • **Possessive pronouns** do not have apostrophes.

      *The course is famous for **its** success.*
└─────────────────────────────────────────────────────────────────┘
```

Write a pronoun to take the place of the underlined words.

1. <u>Mario and I</u> took swimming lessons last summer. _____

2. <u>The lessons</u> lasted for six weeks. _____

3. A local hotel loaned us <u>the hotel's</u> pool. _____

4. <u>The pool</u> was almost olympic size. _____

5. <u>The instructor</u> was a teacher from our school. _____

6. He helped <u>Mario and me</u> to relax in the water. _____

7. <u>Mario and I</u> were swimming in no time. _____

8. We were able to keep up with the rest
   <u>of the class</u>. _____

9. Everyone was surprised at <u>Mario</u> for taking the
   course. _____

10. <u>His family and friends</u> talked him into it. _____

10  **McGraw-Hill Language Arts**
Grade 4, Unit 5, Pronouns,
pages 364–365

**At Home:** Write about something you learned to do.
Include at least three sentences that have pronouns.

78

# Study Skills: Dictionary

A **dictionary** shows the spelling, meaning, and pronunciation of words.

- **Guide words** indicate the first and last words on a page. They appear at the top of each dictionary page.
- A **pronunciation key** shows how to say words. It usually appears at the bottom of every other page.
- **Entry words** are the words explained in the dictionary. They appear in alphabetical order.
- Every entry word includes:
    the **pronunciation** of the word
    the **part of speech** (shown as an abbreviation, like *n., v., adj., adv.*— noun, verb, adjective, adverb)
    one or more **definitions** (sometimes with **example sentences**).

Use the part of the dictionary page below to answer the questions. Underline the correct answer.

> **foil** (foil) *n.* **1.** a very thin sheet of metal. **2.** something that makes another thing seem better when compared [Martha acted as a *foil* when she shouted out the correct answer before Henry could be called on.] **3.** a thin sword with a guard over the point to prevent injury when used in fencing.

1. Which pair of words could be the guide words on this dictionary page?

    fly /folk                fluffy/focus

2. What does the letter *n* stand for in the dictionary entry?

    no pronunciation available      the word is a noun

3. How many definitions are there for the word *foil*?

    2                          3

4. Where would you look to find the pronunciation key?

    on bottom of this or the next page

    next to the guide words

5. Which definition of *foil* has an example sentence?      1      2      3

---

**At Home:** Write an example sentence for a definition of *foil* that doesn't appear in the entry of this page.

**79**

**McGraw-Hill Language Arts**
**Grade 4, Unit 5, Study Skills,**
**pages 372–373**

`5`

# Vocabulary: Homophones and Homographs

---

- **Homophones** are pairs of words that sound alike but are spelled differently and mean different things.
  fare/fair    cents/sense    minor/miner    scene/seen

- **Homographs** are words that are spelled alike but have different meanings. They may be pronounced differently, too.
  *I opened the **trunk** of the car.      The elephant's **trunk** would not fit.
  The tree **trunk** was in our way.*

---

Underline the two words in each sentence that are either homophones or homographs. Then write *homophones* or *homographs* to tell what kind of words they are.

1. It isn't fair that I can't show my pet pig at the fair. _____

2. My eyes were tearing as I began tearing up my entry fee. _____

3. "Bye," I said to the judge as she passed by. _____

4. "Would you help me cut this pile of wood?" asked my grandfather. _____

5. "My saw was here a minute ago, I know I saw it." _____

6. "Next week I will cut the weak tree limb." _____

7. "I can go get you a sandwich and a can of soda." _____

8. "Stay here, Gramps," I said, "I can hear the food vendor coming this way." _____

9. When we were just about through, Dad threw an old flour sack at my feet. _____

10. They're all waiting for their champion sack racer," he said. "Let's all go." _____

---

**McGraw-Hill Language Arts**
**Grade 4, Unit 5, Vocabulary,**
**pages 374–375**

**At Home:** Write five sentences with the word *run*. Each use of the word should have a different meaning.

# Composition: Writing Dialogue

- Dialogue is the part of a story that shows the conversation among characters.
- The exact words a character says have **quotation marks** around them.
- The first word inside of an opening quotation mark is **capitalized.**
- End punctuation appears before a closing quotation mark.
- Words like *said Winston* or *she explained* help the reader know which character is speaking the words in a dialogue.
- Every time a different character speaks, begin a new paragraph.

  Tommy explained**, "T**his is a model of an early airplane.**"** Then he asked Sara**, "D**o you like it**?"**
  Sara exclaimed**, "It**'s wonderful. May I help you build your next model, Tommy**?"**
  **"O**f course you can. We'll have a great time**,"** Tommy said.

Read the story. Underline every group of words spoken by story characters.

**1.-10.** Raymond pushed the door open slowly and said, "Mom, how will I know which puppy to choose?"

   Mrs. Botera thought for a minute and answered, "It's not an easy decision. I think, though, that you'll just know which puppy is right as soon as you meet it." She followed Raymond through the door into a hall lined with kennel cages. "Look, Raymond, a puppy with black spots!" Mrs. Botera directed her son's attention.

   Raymond saw the dog and said, "It looks like our old dog Jed." Raymond asked the attendant to let him see the white puppy with the black spots. "The spots are smaller, but this dog seems just as friendly as good old Jed," Raymond added.

   "The dog is a Dalmatian," the attendant told Raymond as the puppy tumbled into Raymond's arms. "It needs to run a lot, but it can be a wonderful pet."

   Raymond said, "I'll run with it every day because I'm on my school's track team." He and his mother petted the little dog. Raymond thought for awhile. "Let's call him Jed II!" he exclaimed.

**At Home:** Write dialogue that shows a conversation you might have with someone about choosing a new pet. Remember to follow the rules for dialogue from the box on this page.

**McGraw-Hill Language Arts**
**Grade 4, Unit 5, Composition Skills,**
**pages 376–377** 10

McGraw-Hill School Division

# Adverbs That Tell *How*

## RULES

• An **adverb** is a word that tells more about a verb. Adverbs can tell how something happened. Many adverbs end in *-ly*.

*Earthquakes <u>happen</u> **suddenly.***
/ \
**verb** **adverb** (tells how)

Write the adverb that describes each underlined verb.

1. An earthquake really <u>scares</u> most people. _____

2. Scientists can rarely <u>tell</u> when one will strike. _____

3. Earthquakes generally <u>occur</u> along faults. _____

4. Mom <u>described</u> it simply as a large crack in the bedrock. _____

5. Rocks normally <u>move</u> in opposite directions

along a fault. _____

6. Pressure easily <u>builds</u> as rocks push against one another. _____

7. Pressure suddenly <u>releases</u> when one rock

slips past the other. _____

8. The sudden release of energy usually <u>causes</u> vibrations. _____

9. The vibrations <u>travel</u> quickly in waves. _____

10. In California, vibrations or tremors <u>occur</u> regularly. _____

11. The ground <u>vibrates</u> slowly. _____

12. Unsecured things quickly <u>fall</u> to the ground. _____

13. Some broken gas lines <u>explode</u> violently. _____

14. People clearly <u>understand</u> the dangers an

earthquake may bring. _____

15. They wisely <u>prepare</u> ahead of time by learning

good safety rules. _____

**McGraw-Hill Language Arts**
Grade 4, Unit 6, Adverbs,
pages 420–421
15

**At Home:** Choose any five adverbs that you wrote above and use them in sentences. Say your sentences aloud to a member of your family.

82

# Adverbs That Tell *When* or *Where*

> **RULES**
>
> • You already know that an **adverb** tells more about a verb, such as **how** something happened. An adverb can also tell **where** or **when** an action takes place.
>
>  *Kara, drive **slowly!*** (how)
>  *Look **outside.*** (where)
>  *The trees are changing colors **now.*** (when)

Underline the adverb in each sentence. Write whether the adverb tells *when, where,* or *how* about the action that is taking place.

1. The end of summer comes quickly. _____

2. Breezes carry the fallen leaves far. _____

3. Many people enjoy activities outdoors. _____

4. Apples, gourds, and pumpkins are in orchards nearby. _____

5. Travelers also plan car trips then. _____

6. Motorists drive slowly in the countryside. _____

7. Colorful trees appear everywhere. _____

8. Maple leaves often turn bright orange or red. _____

9. Sometimes they turn bright yellow. _____

10. People always enjoy the brilliant colors. _____

11. The colorful leaves do not stay forever. _____

12. Soon the trees are bare. _____

13. Colder weather will come soon. _____

14. Heavy snows will fall later. _____

15. People usually stay indoors during a big snowstorm. _____

**At Home:** Rewrite three of the above sentences using different adverbs. For example: *Heavy snows will fall soon.*

McGraw-Hill Language Arts
Grade 4, Unit 6, Adverbs,
pages 422–423

15

# Adverbs That Compare

• **Adverbs** can be used to make comparisons.

• Add *-er* to short adverbs to compare two actions. Add *-est* to compare more than two actions.

  *Stephanie swims **fast** at practice.*
  *Stephanie swims **faster** than Paula.*
  *Stephanie swims **fastest** of all the swimmers on the team.*

Write the adverb in parentheses that correctly completes the sentence.

**1.** I joined the swim team _____ this year than I did last

  year. (later, latest)

**2.** Swim team fees dropped _____ than they were last

  year. (lowest, lower)

**3.** Our team, the Sharks, practices _____ in the morning

  than the Waves team. (earliest, earlier)

**4.** The Sharks practice _____ than the Waves. (longer, longest)

**5.** Of all the practices and meets, most teams swim _____

  at a championship meet. (harder, hardest)

**6.** Jessica does the butterfly stroke _____ than Yolanda.

  (slower, slowest)

**7.** Our best swimmers kick _____. (harder, hardest)

**8.** Backstroke swimmers who have long strokes swim _____

  than those with short strokes. (fastest, faster)

**9.** Olympic stars swim _____ of all. (fastest, faster)

**10.** Many champions begin training _____ than average

  swimmers. (sooner, soonest)

**McGraw-Hill Language Arts**
**Grade 4, Unit 6, Adverbs,**
**pages 424–425**
10

**At Home:** Tell a family member how you knew which adverb to choose for your answer in the above sentences.

84

# More Adverbs That Compare

> **RULES**
>
> • The words *more* and *most* are usually used to form comparisons with adverbs that end in *-ly* and with longer adverbs.
>
> • Use *more* to compare two actions.
>
>   *A river raft changes its course* **more abruptly** *in rapids than in a gentle stream.*
>
> • Use *most* to compare more than two actions.
>
>   *Of all white water, class VI rapids churn* **most powerfully.**

Underline the word in parentheses that completes each sentence correctly.

1. Water flows (more, most) slowly on level ground than in the mountains.

2. Mountain streams flow (more, most) quickly of all.

3. The Gauley River in West Virginia runs (more, most) swiftly than the Ocoee River in Tennessee.

4. River guides paddle (more, most) cautiously through rapids than through other moving water.

5. Of all times, rafters smile (more, most) happily at the end of a safe trip.

6. Compared with all other sports enthusiasts, kayakers play (more, most) dangerously.

7. Kayakers paddle (more, most) vigorously than rafters.

8. A well-trained guide travels the river (more, most) easily of all river runners.

9. Some river outfitters operate (more, most) safely than others.

10. Of all sports groups, they train their employees (more, most) rigorously.

McGraw-Hill School Division

---

**At Home:** Write two original sentences using adverbs with the words *more* and *most*.

**McGraw-Hill Language Arts**
**Grade 4, Unit 6, Adverbs,**
**pages 426–427**

85

10

# Mechanics and Usage: *Good* and *Well*

┌─ **RULES** ────────────────────────────────────────────

- Use the adjective ***good*** when describing a noun.

  *It is wise to make **good** decisions.*

- Use the adverb ***well*** when telling more about a verb.

  *You will do **well** if you make wise decisions.*

└────────────────────────────────────────────────────────

Write the letter **C** before the sentence that uses *good* or *well* correctly.

1. _____ Ryan's parents are glad that he makes good choices.

   _____ Ryan's parents are glad that he makes well choices.

2. _____ His teachers say he listens good at school.

   _____ His teachers say he listens well at school.

3. _____ They noticed that he chooses friends good.

   _____ They noticed that he chooses friends well.

4. _____ His parents agree that he has good friends.

   _____ His parents agree that he has well friends.

5. _____ They also think that his grades are good.

   _____ They also think that his grades are well.

6. _____ He remembers good in history class, but not in math.

   _____ He remembers well in history class, but not in math.

7. _____ His idea about doing homework in study hall was a good one.

   _____ His idea about doing homework in study hall was a well one.

8. _____ He eats at least three good meals a day and gets plenty of rest.

   _____ He eats at least three well meals a day and gets plenty of rest.

9. _____ Ryan should expect a well report card.

   _____ Ryan should expect a good report card.

10. _____ His teachers and parents are happy that he is progressing so good.

    _____ His teachers and parents are happy that he is progressing so well.

**At Home:** Write a sentence that tells what you do well. Then write a sentence that tells what is good about it. For example: *I ride a bike well. Riding a bike gives me good exercise.*

# Mixed Review

> **RULES**
>
> • An **adverb** tells more about a verb. Adverbs tell *how, when,* or *where* an action takes place.
>
> | | |
> |---|---|
> | We **gladly** went to the county fair. | **tells how** |
> | I **never** miss going with my friends. | **tells when** |
> | It is held **here** every year in the fall. | **tells where** |
>
> • Add *-er* to short adverbs to compare two actions. Add *-est* to compare more than two actions.
>
> My horse jumped **higher** than her horse.
>
> Of all the horses, this one jumped the **highest**.
>
> • The words *more* and *most* are usually used to form comparisons with longer adverbs and adverbs that end in *-y* .
>
> This horse ran **more quickly** than that horse.
>
> Of all the horses, this one ran the **most quickly**.

Circle the adverb that correctly completes each sentence. Write whether the adverb tells *how, when,* or *where.*

1. Our county fair usually attracts many people. _____

2. I arrived earlier at the fair than my friend Emma. _____

3. We gleefully watch many of the events. _____

4. Mike eats the most in the hot dog eating contest. _____

5. The pig race draws a large crowd here. _____

6. Mr. Jenson's pig runs the most quickly of all. _____

7. Mark confidently enters the frog jumping contest. _____

8. The frog that jumps the farthest of all wins a prize. _____

9. My frog never wins the jumping contest. _____

10. We left the fair more reluctantly than we did last year. _____

**At Home:** Talk to family members or friends about the most unusual contest they have seen. Write a paragraph about it. Circle each adverb you include.

87

McGraw-Hill School Division

**McGraw-Hill Language Arts**
**Grade 4, Unit 6, Mixed Review,**
**pages 430–431**

/10

# Negatives

┌─ **RULES** ──────────────────────────────────────────┐

- **Negatives** are words that mean "no." Usually they contain the word *no* or a contraction for *not,* such as: *not, nobody, nowhere, none, no one.*
- Never use more than one negative at a time in a sentence.

  **INCORRECT:** *I **can't** make **no** decisions.*
  **CORRECT:**   *I **can't** make any decisions.*

└──────────────────────────────────────────────────────┘

Underline the double negatives in each sentence. Then rewrite the sentence correctly by replacing one of the negatives with the word in parentheses.

1. There isn't nothing worse than being the new kid at school. (is)

   _____

2. It feels like I'm not never going to make any friends. (ever)

   _____

3. I thought I told you I didn't know nobody at school. (anybody)

   _____

4. I guess that nobody listens to me no more. (anymore)

   _____

5. By now you should understand why I can't invite no one over. (anyone)

   _____

6. You know I don't like going nowhere alone. (anywhere)

   _____

7. There aren't no teachers around to help make the introductions. (are)

   _____

8. Isn't there nothing I can do about this? (something)

   _____

9. I am not trying nothing new until I make at least one new friend. (anything)

   _____

10. We aren't moving nowhere ever again! (anywhere)

    _____

**McGraw-Hill Language Arts**
**Grade 4, Unit 6, Adverbs,**
**pages 432–433**
10

**At Home:** Rewrite sentences 1, 5, and 7 a different way without changing the meaning. Replace the other negative instead.

88

# Prepositions

┌─ **RULES** ─────────────────────────────────────────────┐

• A **preposition** is a word that comes before a noun or a pronoun and relates it to another word in a sentence. Here are some prepositions:

| | | | | |
|---|---|---|---|---|
| *about* | *over* | *from* | *in* | *for* |
| *above* | *under* | *through* | *across* | |
| *after* | *behind* | *until* | *on* | |
| *by* | *near* | *with* | *off* | |

└──────────────────────────────────────────────────────────┘

Underline the preposition in each sentence.

1. Lisa decided she would wear a red sweater over her blouse.

2. First, she looked in the dresser where she keeps her sweaters.

3. She found her red sweater with the others.

4. It was under her favorite blue sweater.

5. Then she spotted her gray sweater across the room.

6. The beautiful gray sweater was sitting on the floor.

7. This sweater was a gift from her Aunt Marge.

8. Aunt Marge would be disappointed if she knew about this.

9. Lisa quickly lifted the sweater off the floor.

10. For a brief moment, Lisa thought she would wear the gray sweater.

11. Lisa donned the sweater and then looked in the mirror.

12. She decided the gray sweater didn't look good with this outfit.

13. She tied the red sweater around her waist.

14. Lisa turned and looked at her reflection again.

15. This is exactly what Lisa would wear to the school dance.

**At Home:** Write several versions of sentence three. Each time, use a different preposition and noun or pronoun to tell where she found the red sweater. For example, *She found her red sweater **on the bed**.*

89

**McGraw-Hill Language Arts**
**Grade 4, Unit 6, Adverbs,**
**pages 434–435**

15

McGraw-Hill School Division

# Prepositional Phrases

┌─ **RULES** ─────────────────────────────────────┐

• A **prepositional phrase** is a group of words that begins with a preposition and ends with a noun or pronoun.

*There are many hot springs and geysers **inside** the park.*

└──────────────────────────────────────────────────┘

Write the prepositional phrase and underline the noun or pronoun that it ends with.

1. Our family went to Yellowstone National Park.

_____

2. Our best friends traveled with us. _____

3. First, we flew a plane into Salt Lake City. _____

4. Then we borrowed a rental van from an agency. _____

5. We spent about a day exploring the Great Salt Lake. _____

6. The huge lake was filled with shrimp. _____

7. We left and headed for Wyoming. _____

8. Driving across Utah was interesting. _____

9. Next we passed through Idaho. _____

10. We finally arrived in a town called Jackson. _____

11. Jackson, Wyoming, is the home of Grand Teton National Park.

_____

12. Yellowstone National Park is north of this area. _____

13. We headed toward the Tetons. _____

14. We arrived at Yellowstone. _____

15. Once inside the park, we visited Old Faithful and other interesting volcanic

features. _____

**McGraw-Hill Language Arts**
Grade 4, Unit 6, Adverbs,
pages 436–437

**At Home:** List the prepositions you wrote in the above exercises.

90

# Combining Sentences: Complex Sentences

> **RULES**
>
> - A **complex sentence** contains two related sentences that have been combined with a conjunction other than *and*, *but*, or *or*.
> - You can combine two short sentences to form a complex sentence.
>   *Some people harvest saguaro fruit. It makes good preserves.*
>   *Some people harvest saguaro fruit because it makes good preserves.*

Combine the short sentences into one complex sentence by using a conjuction from the box. Don't forget correct punctutation.

| because | before | although | if | unless | until |
|---------|--------|----------|-----|--------|-------|
| | wherever | when | while | | |

1. You will see the desert. You travel to Arizona.

   _____

2. Be sure to go on a hike. You are there.

   _____

3. You will see cactus. You hike in the desert.

   _____

4. Bring bottled water. There is no water available.

   _____

5. I never saw a saguaro cactus. I visited Tucson.

   _____

6. You may not see this cactus. You go there.

   _____

7. The saguaro looks like a barrel. It is very young.

   _____

8. Arms don't grow. The cactus is more mature.

   _____

9. They have flowers and fruit. Saguaros don't have leaves.

   _____

10. Desert creatures eat its ripe pulp. The fruit splits open.

   _____

**At Home:** Find a complex sentence in a local newspaper.
Break it down into two separate sentences.

91

**McGraw-Hill Language Arts**
**Grade 4, Unit 6, Adverbs,**
**pages 438–439**  10

McGraw-Hill School Division

# Mechanics and Usage: Commas

**RULES**

- A **comma** shows a pause in your writing.
  *No, I didn't realize the five senses are part of our nervous system.*

- Use a comma to set off the name of the person you are speaking to.
  *David, didn't you listen in health class?*

- Use a comma to set off an introductory word.
  *Well, it's time you started to pay attention.*

Insert commas where needed.

1. Betsy don't touch that hot stove!

2. Phillip why are you shouting at me?

3. Well you were about to burn your fingers!

4. Yes but I would have pulled my hand quickly away.

5. Sure but not quickly enough to keep from getting hurt.

6. Thank you for caring enough to warn me Phillip.

7. Did you know Betsy that your fingertips can send a message to your brain?

8. Yes but how does the message get there?

9. The messages travel through special nerve cells called neurons Betsy.

10. That sounds interesting Phillip.

11. For example neurons in your fingers sense that the stove is hot.

12. Next the message is translated as an electronic impulse.

13. Phillip that sounds amazing!

14. Finally the impulse travels across a network of nerve cells all the way to your brain.

15. Yes I've heard that's how it works.

**McGraw-Hill Language Arts**
Grade 4, Unit 6, Adverbs,
pages 440–441

**At Home:** Ask a family member to use your name as they speak directly to you. Write the first few sentences of your conversation.

15

92

McGraw-Hill School Division

# Mixed Review

- A **negative** means "no." Never use two negatives in one sentence.

    *I have ~~not~~ **never** been on an airplane.*

- A **preposition,** such as *about, of, with, to, through, upon,* comes before a noun or pronoun and links it to the rest of the sentence.

    *The airport was full **of** people.*

- A **prepositional phrase** is a group of words that begins with a preposition and ends in a noun or pronoun.

    *I walked eagerly **toward the plane**.*

- A **complex sentence** combines two ideas by using words that tell where, when, why, how, and under what circumstances.

    *I was very excited. I walked onto the plane.*
    *I was very excited **when** I walked onto the plane.*

**A.** Combine each pair of sentences into a complex sentence. Correct any double negatives.

**1.** I was worried about flying. I was in the air.

_____

**2.** I couldn't never tell we were moving. We flew through the sky.

_____

**3.** We landed smoothly. We reached our destination.

_____

**4.** I don't never like to fly. The weather is bad.

_____

**5.** I enjoy flying. It is very exciting for me.

_____

**B. 6.-10.** Underline five prepositional phrases in the complex sentences you wrote.

**At Home:** Think about when you did something for the first time. Write a paragraph describing what it was like. Circle each prepositional phrase you use. Check to see if you can combine any sentences.

**McGraw-Hill Language Arts**
**Grade 4, Unit 6, Mixed Review,**
**pages 442–443**

10

McGraw-Hill School Division

# Common Errors: Adverbs

McGraw-Hill School Division

┌─ **RULES** ─────────────────────────────────────────────┐

• An **adjective** describes a noun. An **adverb** tells more about a verb.

 *I put the **little** puzzle together **quickly.***

• ***Good*** is an adjective. ***Well*** is an adverb.

 *My **good** friend and I work **well** together.*

• Do not use two negative words together in a sentence.

 *They could not find ~~no~~ **any** puzzles to do.*

• Many adverbs are formed by adding **-ly** to an adjective. For most adverbs, do not change the spelling of the base word when you add **-ly**.

 *We **finally** found a puzzle we liked.*

└─────────────────────────────────────────────────────────┘

Write the word in parentheses ( ) that completes each sentence correctly.

1. I (recent, recently) finished putting another jigsaw puzzle together.  _____

2. I (frequent, frequently) work on puzzles instead of watching TV.  _____

3. I have (success, successfully) completed many kinds of puzzles.  _____

4. I do not buy (any, no) puzzles that have fewer than a thousand pieces.  _____

5. Three-dimensional puzzles are (good, well) puzzles to put together.  _____

6. Some puzzles (continue, continually) repeat the same picture over and over.  _____

7. They are (especial, especially) hard to put together._____

8. My brother and I work (good, well) together on puzzles.  _____

9. He doesn't have time to work on them (anymore, no more).  _____

10. I feel great when I (final, finally) complete a puzzle._____

**10** **McGraw-Hill Language Arts**
**Grade 4, Unit 6, Adverbs,**
**pages 444–445**

**At Home:** Write about something you like to do. Include at least three sentences that have adverbs.

94

# Study Skills: Encyclopedia

- An **encyclopedia** is a reference work that contains articles on many subjects. It may be a single book, but it is more often a set of books or volumes.

- The volumes in a set of encyclopedias are labeled these two ways: numbers and alphabetically by subject.

- The last volume in an encyclopedia is the index, which lists all the subjects written about in the encyclopedia. The index is also arranged alphabetically by subject.

Complete each sentence with the number of the encyclopedia volume in which you would find an article.

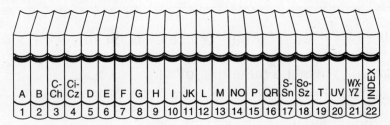

1. An article on the horseshoe crab may be found in volume

_____

2. To find out about coyotes, look in volume

_____

3. Information on the Black Hills may be found in volume

_____

4. Japanese literature may be looked up in volume

_____

5. Radioactivity has an article in volume

_____

6. You will find an article on Catherine the Great in volume

_____

7. An article on Dodge City would be found in volume

_____

8. Read the article about the country of Ethiopia in volume

_____

9. Look up the painter Henri Matisse in volume

_____

10. The article on the author of *Uncle Tom's Cabin,* Harriet Beecher Stowe, may be found in volume

_____

**At Home:** Think of two subjects you would like to learn more about. In what volume of the encyclopedia shown on this page would you look for them?

**95**

**McGraw-Hill Language Arts**
**Grade 4, Unit 6, Study Skills,**
**pages 452–453**

/10

# Vocabulary: Suffixes

- A **suffix** is a word part added to the end of a base word.

  work + er = worker   neat + ness = neatness
  slow + ly = slowly

- A suffix changes the meaning of the base word to which it is added.

| Suffix | Meaning |
|--------|---------|
| -er | person who |
| -ful | full of |
| -ion | an act or state of being |
| -ly | in a certain way |
| -y | like, full of |
| -less | without |
| -ment | the result of |

Underline the word in each sentence that has a suffix. Write an equation for it. (See above for an example.)

1. It is very windy today. _____

2. I am showing my art project to my teacher today. _____

3. Maybe if I walk quickly, my papers won't blow. _____

4. I was successful and made it to class on time. _____

5. My teacher gave me a cheerful greeting. _____

6. When she saw my art work, she expressed amazement. _____

7. First her expression worried me. _____

8. "You used your materials in a wonderful way," she said. _____

9. The bright colors make it look so joyful. _____

10. My parents' encouragement helped me finish my art project. _____

McGraw-Hill School Division

**McGraw-Hill Language Arts**
**Grade 4, Unit 6, Vocabulary,**
**pages 454–455**

**At Home:** Use a dictionary. Find and list words that are formed with the suffix -ist such as *artist*.

# Composition: Outlining

- When you need to organize ideas for a report, you can make an **outline**. Your writing topic is named in the outline **title**.

- The main topics are listed next to Roman numerals followed by periods. (I. II. III.)

- Each main idea will become a paragraph in your report.

- Subtopics are listed with capital letters followed by periods under each main topic. (A. B. C. ) Subtopics are the details that support or explain a main topic in a paragraph.

Here is an outline that Julia prepared for a science report about sound. Complete the outline by writing the correct numerals and letters on the lines.

Title: Sound

**1.–10.**

_____ A Kind of Energy

_____ Sound waves caused by vibrations.

_____ Waves travel at speed of sound.

_____ Characteristics of Sound

_____ Volume

_____ Pitch

_____ Unusual Sound Conditions

_____ SONAR (sound navigation ranging)

_____ Noise pollution

_____ Hearing impairments

**At Home:** Think of a topic for a science report you would like to research. Outline your ideas. Use main topics, subtopics, and Roman numerals. Don't forget a title.

97

**McGraw-Hill Language Arts**
**Grade 4, Unit 6, Composition Skills,**
**pages 456–457**

10

McGraw-Hill School Division

## Sentences

### RULES

- A **sentence** is a group of words that expresses a complete thought. A sentence names the person or thing you are talking about. It also tells what happened.

  SENTENCE: *I received a letter from my pen pal.*

- A **sentence fragment** is a group of words that does not express a complete thought.

  FRAGMENT: *Friends for a long time.*

Read each group of words. Circle **yes** if the words make a sentence. Circle **no** if they are a sentence fragment.

1. Maritza is my favorite pen pal.  (**yes**)  no
2. Lives in Puerto Rico.  **yes**  (**no**)
3. I have been writing to Maritza for two years.  (**yes**)  no
4. She is four months older than me.  (**yes**)  no
5. Tall girl with green eyes.  **yes**  (**no**)
6. We are both in the fourth grade.  (**yes**)  no
7. I visited Puerto Rico with my family.  (**yes**)  no
8. Stayed at Maritza's house.  **yes**  (**no**)
9. Maritza introduced me to all her friends.  (**yes**)  no
10. Sometimes her brother.  **yes**  (**no**)

**At Home:** Choose a sentence fragment from this page. Add words to make it a sentence. Write your new sentence on a separate sheet of paper.

---

## Declarative and Interrogative Sentences

### RULES

- A **declarative sentence** makes a statement.

  It begins with a **capital letter.**    It ends with a **period.**

  *My pen pal lives in Japan.*

- An **interrogative sentence** asks a question.

  It begins with a **capital letter.**    It ends with a **question mark.**

  *Where does your pen pal live?*

Draw one line under each sentence that makes a statement. Draw two lines under each sentence that asks a question.

1. My funny letter is in my pocket.
2. Do you need to buy stamps?
3. I will mail my letter at the post office.
4. Many customers are waiting in line.
5. There are three women and two men behind me.
6. How many packages will be mailed today?
7. What is in the big envelope?
8. It contains postcards from Japan.
9. Sayuri, my pen pal, sends me wonderful presents.
10. Can you think of something she would like from the United States?

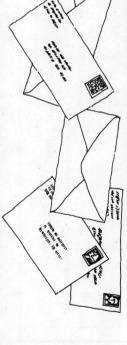

**At Home:** Write two sentences about the state you live in. Then write two questions that you would ask Sayuri about Japan.

# Imperative and Exclamatory Sentences

## RULES

- An **imperative sentence** tells or asks someone to do something.
  It begins with a **capital letter**.

  *Cook the rice and beans for twenty minutes.*  It ends with a **period**.

- An **exclamatory sentence** shows strong feeling.
  It begins with a **capital letter**.

  *What a delicious dinner you prepared!*  It ends with an **exclamation mark**.

Draw one line under each sentence that tells or asks someone to do something. Draw two lines under each sentence that shows strong feeling.

1. Please help set the table.

2. It's surprising how many are coming!

3. Put the flowers on the table.

4. What a mess I made!

5. Don't forget to take out the garbage.

6. Watch for our guests, please.

7. How tired I am!

8. Turn on the radio and close the window.

9. Oh no, I broke a glass!

10. Wow, this is a big party!

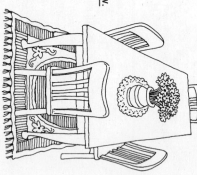

**At Home:** Draw a funny picture. Write three exclamatory sentences to go with your picture.

3

---

McGraw-Hill School Division

# Combining Sentences: Compound Sentences

## RULES

- A compound sentence is made up of two sentences joined by **and**, **or**, or **but**.

- Use a comma (,) before **and**, **or**, or **but** when you write a compound sentence.

  *This is a zoo, **but** animals are not in cages.
  We can visit the new zoo, **or** we can go
  to the planetarium.
  Some keepers feed the zoo animals, **and**
  other people study the animals.*

| Conjunction Box |
|---|
| **and** - links ideas |
| **but** - shows contrast |
| **or** - shows choice |

Underline the conjunction in each compound sentence. Then write it on the line.

1. Natasha and I watched the monkeys,
   but we didn't feed them.

   _____ but

2. Zookeepers know what kind of food each animal
   eats, and they know how much it needs.

   _____ and

3. Wild animals can get their own food, but zoo
   animals must be fed by keepers.

   _____ but

4. Lions don't eat every day in the wild, and they're
   not fed every day in the zoo, either.

   _____ and

5. Next month we will visit a museum, or we will
   go back to the zoo.

   _____ or

**At Home:** Write a pair of sentences with similar ideas and combine them by using the conjunction *or*.

5

## Mechanics and Usage: Sentence Punctuation

### RULES

Every sentence begins with a capital letter.

- A **declarative sentence** makes a statement. It ends with a **period**. *The contest begins Friday night.*
- An **interrogative sentence** asks a question. It ends with a **question mark**. *Who will be the winner?*
- An **imperative sentence** tells or asks someone to do something. It ends with a **period**. *Please sit down.*
- An **exclamatory sentence** shows strong feeling. It ends with an **exclamation mark**. *Hooray, I'm the winner!*
- Add a **comma** and the **conjunction** *and, or,* or *but* to join parts of a compound sentence. *Chaz will play violin tonight, or he will play piano.*

Underline each sentence that is written correctly.

1. When does the contest begin.

2. Oh, the music is lovely!

3. Please be on time for the show.

4. you and I can sit here.

5. Tell me all about the performance.

6. Do you see Marta and John in the audience?

7. Clap for all the performers

8. wow, the trumpet player was fabulous!

9. Simon wanted to come tonight, but he sprained his ankle playing ball.

10. We all gathered in the hallway during intermission.

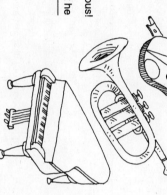

**At Home:** Rewrite correctly the sentences that you didn't underline.

---

## Mixed Review

### RULES

- A **declarative sentence** makes a statement and ends in a period. *I like to go on picnics.*
- An **interrogative sentence** asks a question and ends in a question mark. *Would you like to go on a picnic?*
- An **imperative sentence** tells or asks someone to do something and ends in a period. *Get some hotdogs.*
- An **exclamatory sentence** shows strong feeling and ends in an exclamation point. *What a terrific idea!*
- Use the words *and, but,* or *or* to combine two sentences into a **compound sentence**. Use a comma before the conjunction. *Picnics are fun.* + *You have to plan them well.* *Picnics are fun, but you have to plan them well.*

Circle the word that describes each kind of sentence. Add the correct end punctuation.

1. Would you like to help me plan a picnic?
   declarative    (interrogative)    imperative    exclamatory    compound

2. The weather is going to be perfect.
   (declarative)    interrogative    imperative    exclamatory    compound

3. Call some friends and see if they can come.
   declarative    interrogative    (imperative)    exclamatory    compound

4. The soda was warm, but we drank it anyway.
   declarative    interrogative    imperative    exclamatory    (compound)

5. What a perfect day!
   declarative    interrogative    imperative    (exclamatory)    compound

**At Home:** Imagine having a family picnic. Write five sentences about it. Write one declarative, interrogative, imperative, exclamatory, and compound sentence.

# Complete Subjects and Complete Predicates

**RULES**

- The **complete subject** includes all the words in the subject that tell whom or what the sentence is about.
- The **complete predicate** includes all the words in the predicate that tell what the subject does or is.

*Some children read stories to others.*

←complete subject    complete predicate→

Tell whether the underlined part of the sentence is a complete subject or a complete predicate. Circle your answer.

1. <u>Story Theater</u> is a special kind of storytelling.

   (complete subject)    complete predicate

2. <u>Members of the group</u> are assigned roles.

   (complete subject)    complete predicate

3. The actors <u>read their parts aloud.</u>

   complete subject    (complete predicate)

4. Many readers <u>practice reading with expression.</u>

   complete subject    (complete predicate)

5. They <u>change their voices to sound like the characters.</u>

   complete subject    (complete predicate)

6. Sometimes <u>one reader</u> is assigned only one page.

   (complete subject)    complete predicate

7. <u>Many different kinds of stories</u> can be used in Story Theater.

   (complete subject)    complete predicate

8. <u>The fourth-grade class</u> read "The Courage of Sarah Noble."

   (complete subject)    complete predicate

9. My whole family <u>came to the performance.</u>

   complete subject    (complete predicate)

10. Our reading <u>was a huge success.</u>

    complete subject    (complete predicate)

**At Home:** Choose a story you would like to read aloud to a parent or a sibling. Read the first page aloud. Then identify the complete subject of each sentence.

---

McGraw-Hill School Division

# Simple Subjects

**RULES**

- The **complete subject** includes all the words in the subject that tell whom or what the sentence is about.
- The **simple subject** is the main word in the complete subject. It tells who or what the sentence is about.

*At first hot air was used to fill big round balloons.*

complete subject
↑
simple subject

The complete subject is underlined in each sentence. Write the simple subject on the line.

1. Some <u>inventors</u> hoped that hot-air balloons would become popular. _____ inventors

2. Many <u>people</u> didn't think balloons should be used for transportation. _____ people

3. <u>Floating in air</u> is like floating in water. _____ floating

4. Later, <u>propellers</u> were put on huge, long balloons. _____ propellers

5. Soon special <u>balloons</u> proved to be faster and safer. _____ airplanes

6. Today special <u>balloons</u> are used for sport and to lift weather instruments. _____ balloons

7. My <u>parents</u> took me to an air show. _____ parents

8. Many fantastic <u>photographs</u> were on display. _____ photographs

9. An airplane <u>wing</u> is curved on top and flat on the bottom. _____ wing

10. The Wright brothers' <u>Flyer</u> was the world's first successful airplane. _____ Flyer

**At Home:** Write two sentences about things that fly. Underline the simple subject in each sentence.

## Simple Predicates

**RULES**

- The **complete predicate** includes all the words that tell what the subject does or is.
- The **simple predicate** is the main word in the complete predicate. It tells exactly what the subject does or is.

*Energy gives things power.*

complete predicate

simple predicate

The complete predicate is underlined in each sentence. Write the simple predicate on the line.

1. Your body <u>gets</u> its energy from food.                                  gets

2. The energy <u>keeps</u> you moving.                                         keeps

3. Energy <u>comes</u> from the sun.                                           comes

4. All animals <u>store</u> energy from the sun.                               store

5. Moving things <u>use</u> energy, too.                                        use

6. A gusty wind <u>pushes</u> a sailboat across the water.                     pushes

7. An electric current <u>flows</u> through a wire.                            flows

8. It <u>makes</u> light and heat.                                             makes

9. Often, it <u>runs</u> a machine.                                            runs

10. Electric energy <u>lights</u> our homes.                                    lights

**At Home:** Write two sentences about how you use energy. Underline the simple predicate in each sentence.

10

---

## Combining Sentences: Compound Subjects

**RULES**

- The **compound subject** is two or more simple subjects that have the same predicate. Join simple subjects with **and** or **or.**

Ethan
and          went to the beach.
Ginny

Join the subject of each sentence pair to make a compound subject. Use the word in parentheses ( ).

1. Some joggers run on the sand. A dog runs on the sand. (and)
**Some joggers and a dog run on the sand.**

2. Mom will watch Ethan swim. I will watch Ethan swim. (or)
**Mom or I will watch Ethan swim.**

3. Ginny collected beautiful shells.
Doug collected beautiful shells. (and)
**Ginny and Doug collected beautiful shells.**

4. A pebble is in my shoe. A seashell is in my shoe. (or)
**A pebble or a seashell is in my shoe.**

5. The chairs were set up nearby. The tables were set up nearby. (and)
**The chairs and the tables were set up nearby.**

**At Home:** Write a compound subject to complete this sentence: _____ floated in the water.

## Combining Sentences: Compound Predicates

**RULES**

- The **compound predicate** contains two or more simple predicates that have the same subject. Join the simple predicates with **and, but,** or **or.**

  *We study and rehearse our lines.*

  *Our teacher laughs or cries after each scene.*

  *She wanted but didn't get more funding.*

Join the predicate of each sentence pair to make a compound predicate. Use the word in parentheses ( ).

1. Jeanette sings in the play. Jeanette dances in the play. (and)

   **Jeanette sings and dances in the play.**

2. The actors talk before the opening. The actors rest before the opening. (or)

   **The actors talk or rest before the opening.**

3. The school rented chairs for the performance. The school borrowed chairs for the performance. (and)

   **The school rented and borrowed chairs for the performance.**

4. My teacher didn't ask us to make costumes. My teacher persuaded us to make costumes. (but)

   **My teacher didn't ask but persuaded us to make costumes.**

5. My father didn't sell 20 tickets. My father bought 20 tickets. (but)

   **My father didn't sell but bought 20 tickets.**

5

McGraw-Hill Language Arts
Grade 4, Unit 1, Sentences,
pages 22–23

**At Home:** Write a compound predicate to complete this
sentence: *The audience _____ after the
final act.*

11

---

## Mechanics and Usage: Correcting Run-on Sentences

**RULES**

- A **run-on sentence** contains two or more complete sentences that run together.

  *A stonefish looks like a rock this disguise fools other fish.*

- To fix a run-on sentence, show each complete sentence by using a capital letter and the correct end punctuation.

  *A stonefish looks like a rock. This disguise fools other fish.*

- You can also fix a run-on sentence by rewriting it as a compound sentence.

  *A stonefish looks like a rock, and this disguise fools other fish.*

Tell which sentences are written correctly. Circle **run-on** or **correct.**

1. A stonefish never goes hungry. Its food comes right to it!    run-on    (correct)

2. Looking like a stone helps the stonefish get its food, and it also protects it from other creatures.    run-on    (correct)

3. One kind of fish looks like a clump of seaweed another looks like a piece of coral.    (run-on)    correct

4. A ferocious inhabitant of a coral reef is the moray eel it is an ugly looking creature.    (run-on)    correct

5. A four-inch-long fish swims straight to the eel. It is unaware of any danger.    run-on    (correct)

6. The little fish swims about the eel it often touches the eel.    (run-on)    correct

7. The little fish swims right into the eel's half-opened mouth then it swims out again.    (run-on)    correct

8. The ever-hungry eel did not try to eat the little fish. The eel remains perfectly still.    run-on    (correct)

9. The little fish is like a doctor, and the eel is like a patient.    run-on    (correct)

10. The little fish, called a wrasse, cleans the big fish it rids the big fish of tiny worms and other creatures.    (run-on)    correct

12

McGraw-Hill Language Arts
Grade 4, Unit 1, Sentences,
pages 24–25

**At Home:** Choose a run-on sentence from above and
rewrite it as two complete sentences or a compound
sentence.

10

T6

# Mixed Review

## RULES

- The **complete subject** includes all the words in the subject.

    *Summer camp* offers many summer activities.

- The **complete predicate** includes all the words that tell what the subject does or is.

    Summer camp *offers many summer activities.*

- A **compound subject** has two or more simple subjects that have the same predicate. The simple subjects are joined by *and* or *or*.

    *The girls play sports.    The boys play sports.*

    *The girls **and** boys play sports.*

- A **compound predicate** has two or more simple predicates that have the same subject. The simple predicates are joined by *and*, *but*, or *or*.

    *The campers sleep at the camp.  The campers eat at the camp.*

    *The campers sleep **and** eat at the camp.*

**A.** Underline the complete subject. Circle the complete predicate.

1. Several of my friends (go to summer camp.)

2. The camp (provides many activities.)

3. The campers (learn about the wilderness.)

4. A nature instructor (takes them on daily field trips.)

5. Several nature trails (wind through the camp grounds.)

**B.** Underline the compound subject or circle the compound predicate.

6. Deer and bears live on the camp grounds.

7. The campers (look and listen for the animals.)

8. Crafts and sports are favorite camp activities.

9. Campers (design and make their own projects.)

10. Parents and counselors coach sporting events.

**At Home:** Write five sentences describing your favorite summer activity. Circle the complete subjects. Underline the complete predicates. Include one compound subject and predicate.

☑ 10

McGraw-Hill Language Arts
Grade 4, Unit 1, Mixed Review,
pages 26–27

13

---

# Common Errors: Sentence Fragments and Run-on Sentences

## RULES

- A **sentence fragment** does not express a complete thought.

    *Have a taste of their own.    Dried grapes.*

- Correct a sentence fragment by adding a subject or a predicate.

    *Dried fruits have a taste of their own.    Dried grapes **are called raisins.***

- A **run-on sentence** contains two or more sentences that should stand alone.

    *Plums grow on trees dried plums are called prunes.*

- Correct a run-on sentence by rewriting it as two sentences or as a compound sentence.

    *Plums grow on trees. Dried plums are called prunes.*

Read each group of words. Write *F* if it is a fragment. Write *R* if it is a run-on sentence. Write *S* if it is a complete sentence.

R ___ 1. People grow grapes many grapes are grown in California.

F ___ 2. In warm climates.

R ___ 3. Grapes grow on vines they hang on the vines in bunches.

S ___ 4. Grapes are grown in large fields called vineyards.

R ___ 5. Workers pick the grapes they place the grapes on wooden trays.

F ___ 6. Placed in the sun.

R ___ 7. The wooden trays stay in the sun the sun dries the grapes.

F ___ 8. Become wrinkled and turn a blackish brown.

R ___ 9. The sun dries the grapes the grapes finally turn into raisins.

F ___ 10. Packed and sent to stores and sold.

**At Home:** Change the sentence fragments labeled above to complete sentences or compound sentences.

☑ 10

McGraw-Hill Language Arts
Grade 4, Unit 1, Sentences,
pages 28–29

14

T7

# Study Skills: Note-Taking and Summarizing

- To remember what you have read, **take notes** that include enough words to help you recall important information such as the main ideas and supporting details.
- Write a **summary**, including the main topic and supporting details or facts.

**A.** Read the paragraph about space camp. Then underline the best choice for each item shown below.

Between the months of February and December every year, students attend the United States Space Camp in Huntsville, Alabama. The students come from the United States and countries around the world. Their interests range from math and science to engineering and space flight. They go to classes and see films about flying on the space shuttle. They also visit the space flight center. At the center, students get hands-on experience with model rockets and simulators, which allow them to become familiar with the weightlessness of space. The high point of the week-long camp is the space shuttle mission simulation, which includes launching and landing of the shuttle.

1. Topic:
   a. Huntsville, Alabama
   b. United States Space Camp

2. Main Idea:
   a. one week between February and December
   b. students learn about space shuttle flights

3. Supporting Detail:
   a. films, classes, visit to space flight center
   b. students have different interests

4. Supporting Detail:
   a. people are weightless in space
   b. space shuttle mission simulation with launch and landing

**B.** Write a summary about the paragraph. **Answers may vary.**

5. **The United States Space Camp allows students from the U.S. and around the world to know what it is like to travel on the space shuttle. They spend one week at the camp, attending classes, viewing films, and visiting the space flight center. A simulated space shuttle flight with a launch and landing caps off the week.**

5
McGraw-Hill Language Arts
Grade 4, Unit 1, Study Skills,
pages 36–37

At Home: Write notes for a section of a textbook or an encyclopedia article you read. Include a topic, main idea, and supporting details.

15

---

# Vocabulary: Time-Order Words

- **Time-order words** can help you understand in what order things happen in a story. These kinds of words can help you when you are following a set of directions or learning about an event.

  after   afterwards   this afternoon   before   as soon as   finally   first
  later   last   next   meanwhile   then   tomorrow   right now   yesterday

Circle the time-order word that will complete each sentence correctly.

1. The (first/finally) thing this morning, Mom told me I had to clean my room.

2. (Then/Meanwhile) she told me I had to finish my homework.

3. (Tomorrow/Finally) she said I could work on my computer.

4. (Later/Now) in the day my dad asked if I wanted to play catch with him.

5. I said, "(As soon as/Next) I finish this e-mail."

6. (After/Later) I signed off, I got my catcher's mitt.

7. My dad said, "I am going to give you a workout (a long time ago/this afternoon)."

8. "Sure, sure," I teased, "just like you did (today/yesterday)."

9. "(Right now/Later) you are throwing very well," said Dad.

10. "Maybe (this morning/tomorrow) we'll work on hitting the ball."

16
McGraw-Hill Language Arts
Grade 4, Unit 1, Vocabulary,
pages 38–39

At Home: Think about how using time-order words in directions helps you. Then write a set of directions explaining how to get from your house to school.

10

## Composition: Main Idea

- A **paragraph** is a group of sentences that tell about a **main idea**. The main idea tells what the writing is about.
- A paragraph should include:
  A **topic sentence** that states the main idea.
  **Supporting details** that clarify and develop the main idea.
- To connect ideas within a paragraph, use time-order words.
- If a sentence does not contain a detail that supports the main idea, take it out.

For each paragraph below, the topic sentence with a main idea appears in dark type. Some of the other sentences of the paragraph contain supporting details. Other sentences contain details that do not support the main idea. Underline the detail sentences that do not support the main ideas.

**1.–2. I found an old box yesterday.** It was lying on the floor of our attic. At first, I thought it was trash. My house has a basement and a garage. I was about to throw the old box away. Then, I heard a jiggling sound when I picked it up. So, I opened the lid. There were at least one hundred photographs of my father from long, long ago inside of the box. It's so interesting to see what he looked like when he was about my age. I called my friend to see if she wanted to come over for dinner.

**3.–4. Stacey and I went skating on the pond yesterday.** First, our parents tested the ice to make sure it was solid and safe. In the summer, I swim in the pond. We put on our skates and took off over the ice. First, Stacey skated backwards around the rim of the pond. Next, I skated to the center of the pond and spun around like a top. Have you seen tops whose colors blur when they spin? After an hour of skating, Stacey and I collapsed, tired but happy. Finally, my mother gave us each a cup of hot cocoa from a thermos.

**5. I will never forget my first airplane ride.** The captain spoke over a loud-speaker. He welcomed everyone on board. Who invented the airplane? Then, he asked us all to put on our seat belts and make sure our seats were in their upright position. The engines roared, and the plane began to move. As the plane lifted off the runway, it felt like my heart rose up out of my body, too!

⬚ 5
McGraw-Hill Language Arts
Grade 4, Unit 1, Composition Skills,
pages 40–41

**At Home:** Write a topic sentence for a paragraph that tells about the first time you did something special. Then, write sentences with three or more supporting details to complete the paragraph.

17

---

## Nouns

**RULES**

- A noun names a person, place, or thing.
  | | |
  |---|---|
  | **person:** | *teacher* |
  | **place:** | *school* |
  | **thing:** | *book* |
- A **noun** may name more than one person, place, or thing.
  *teacher-teachers  book-books  school-schools*

Underline the nouns in each sentence. Then write each noun on the chart under the correct heading. Some headings will have fewer than seven nouns.

1. <u>Mr. Finney</u> taught <u>history</u> at <u>Central School</u>.

2. His <u>students</u> were encouraged to bring in interesting <u>articles</u> about foreign <u>countries</u>.

3. Usually, the <u>teacher</u> had an interesting historical <u>fact</u> to tell about the <u>news</u>.

4. The older <u>children</u> enjoyed the <u>stories</u> that were shared in his <u>classroom</u>.

5. His amusing <u>tales</u> usually made his <u>listeners</u> laugh.

| PERSONS | PLACES | THINGS |
|---|---|---|
| Mr. Finney | Central School | history |
| students | countries | articles |
| teacher | classroom | fact |
| children | | news |
| listeners | | stories |
| | | tales |

⬚ 5
McGraw-Hill Language Arts
Grade 4, Unit 2, Nouns,
pages 88–89

**At Home:** Think of a sentence with nouns that are the names of a person, a place, and a thing. Write each noun in the blank spaces under the correct heading on the chart.

18

## Worksheet 19

Name _____ Date _____

**Reteach** | 19 |

# Singular and Plural Nouns

## RULES

- A **singular noun** names one person, place, or thing.
- A **plural noun** names two or more persons, places, or things.
- To identify **singular** or **plural nouns** it may be helpful to test a word with the questions: *Can you see one ____? Can you see two ____?*
- Add -s to most nouns to form the plural.

  one *boy* → two *boys*

- Add -es to form the plural of nouns ending in *s, x, ch,* or *sh.*

  one *bus* → two *buses*

  one *box* → two *boxes*

  one *church* → two *churches*

  one *bush* → two *bushes*

Underline the correct plural form of each noun and write it on the line.

1. cup      (cups, cupes, cupps) — <u>cups</u>
2. plate     (plats, plaets, plates) — <u>plates</u>
3. house    (housse, houses, houzes) — <u>houses</u>
4. box      (boxes, boxs, boxis) — <u>boxes</u>
5. stitch    (stitchis, stitchs, stitches) — <u>stitches</u>
6. boss     (bosses, bosss, boses) — <u>bosses</u>
7. scratch   (scratched, scratches, scratchs) — <u>scratches</u>
8. bush     (busses, bushes, bushs) — <u>bushes</u>
9. light     (lights, lightes, lites) — <u>lights</u>
10. candle   (candels, candls, candles) — <u>candles</u>

19

**At Home:** Write a list of nouns that name equipment and people you might expect to find on a playground.

McGraw-Hill Language Arts
Grade 4, Unit 2, Nouns,
pages 90–91

| 10 |

---

## Worksheet 20

Name _____ Date _____

**Reteach** | 20 |

# Nouns Ending with y

## RULES

- When forming the plural of nouns ending in *y*:

  Change the *y* to *i* and add -es if the noun ends in a consonant + *y*.

  one *baby* → two *babies*

  Just add -s if the noun ends in a vowel + *y*.

  one *day* → two *days*

Write the correct plural noun in parentheses to complete each sentence.

1. Elliott heard that I got two new __**puppies**__ last month. (puppys/puppies)
2. They were a special gift for my brother's and my __**birthdays**__. (birthdays/ birthdayes)
3. I had to wait several __**Mondays**__ before receiving my new pets. (Mondays, Mondais)
4. We had to travel through a few different __**cities**__ to get them. (citys, cities)
5. No __**subways**__ could transport us that far. (subwayes, subways)
6. We traveled on two __**ferries**__ to get to the pet store and back. (ferrys, ferries)
7. There were several __**varieties**__ of pets at the store. (varietys, varieties)
8. I was surprised to find some __**monkeys**__ there for sale. (monkeys, monkies)
9. My new puppies are different from the __**kitties**__ I once had. (kittys, kitties)
10. It will take many __**days**__ before they are properly trained. (daies, days)

20

**At Home:** Write sentences using five of the plural nouns from the above exercise. Read your sentences aloud to a family member.

McGraw-Hill Language Arts
Grade 4, Unit 2, Nouns,
pages 92–93

| 10 |

McGraw-Hill School Division

## More Plural Nouns

**RULES**

- Some nouns do not add -s or -es to form the plural.
- Some nouns have special plural forms.

  one *man* → two *men*
  one *child* → two *children*

- Some nouns have the same singular and plural forms.

  one *moose* → two *moose*
  one *deer* → two *deer*

Write the irregular plural noun from the box that completes each sentence.

| | |
|---|---|
| one woman → two women | one deer → two deer |
| one tooth → two teeth | one mouse → two mice |
| one goose → two geese | one fisherman → two fishermen |
| one scissors → two scissors | one fish → two fish |
| one foot → two feet | one trout → two trout |

1. My father helped me learn how to use a fly rod to catch ___fish___.

2. It is a challenge to catch brook and rainbrow ___trout___ without live bait.

3. My dad and I stood as quiet as two ___mice___ near the edge of the stream.

4. It is impossible to go fly fishing without getting your ___feet___ wet.

5. Most fly ___fishermen___ wear special fishing boots called waders.

6. They also wear vests with pockets for small tools like pliers and ___scissors___.

7. Without scissors, they would have to bite with their ___teeth___ to cut the line.

8. Many ___women___ also enjoy the sport of fly fishing.

9. On our last trip, we encountered several ___deer___ getting drinks of water.

10. We also enjoyed seeing flocks of ___geese___ migrating overhead.

McGraw-Hill Language Arts
Grade 4, Unit 2, Nouns,
pages 94–95

**At Home:** Make up a sentence for each plural noun in the chart above. Say each sentence to a parent or sibling.

10

---

## Common and Proper Nouns

**RULES**

- **Common nouns** name people, places, or things.
- **Proper nouns** name particular people, places, or things and always begin with a capital letter.

  *The scientific name for an animal in North America is the same in Europe.*

Underline common nouns and write any proper nouns that appear.

1. Red Cliff High School began classes in August, before Labor Day.
   ___Red Cliff High School, August, Labor Day___

2. We learned about scientific classification in Biology 101 last November.
   ___Biology 101, November___

3. We studied that topic until the Wednesday before Thanksgiving.
   ___Wednesday, Thanksgiving___

4. Many centuries ago, a philosopher from Greece named Aristotle developed a way to classify living organisms. ___Greece, Aristotle___

5. Aristotle grouped animals according to whether they had red blood.
   ___Aristotle___

6. A scientist named John Ray classified living organisms by their species.
   ___John Ray___

7. This biologist from England noticed that members of the same species can breed together. ___England___

8. About a century later, Carolus Linnaeus developed the classification system we use today. ___Carolus Linnaeus___

9. Linnaeus was born in the city of Kristianstad, Sweden, in 1707.
   ___Linnaeus, Kristianstad, Sweden___

10. He first explained his system in a book titled *Species Plantarum*.
    ___Species Plantarum___

McGraw-Hill Language Arts
Grade 4, Unit 2, Nouns,
pages 96–97

**At Home:** Write the days of the week and months of the year in order. Read your lists to a family member.

10

## Mechanics and Usage: Capitalization

**RULES**

- **Proper nouns,** including names of **days, months,** and **holidays,** always begin with a capital letter.

  Tuesday     February     St. Valentine's Day

- Capitalize **family names** that refer to specific people. Also capitalize **titles of respect** that are part of a specific name.

  *Mother* spoke to my teacher, *Miss Meg Hargrove.*

- Capitalize the first word and all important words in the **title** of a book, magazine, song, poem, play, short story, or movie.

  *My favorite play is Fiddler on the Roof.*

Read each pair of sentences. Write the letter *C* before the sentence that is correctly written.

1. ___C___ Dad recently read a book to my brother Ryan called *Customs Around the World for Holidays.*

   _____ Dad recently read a book to my brother Ryan called *Customs around the World For Holidays.*

2. ___C___ In the United States, the last Monday in may is called memorial Day.

   _____ In the United States, the last Monday in May is called Memorial Day.

3. _____ On that day, miss lauren connolly attends a parade in Northville, michigan, with her Father and Mother.

   ___C___ On that day, Miss Lauren Connolly attends a parade in Northville, Michigan, with her father and mother.

4. ___C___ Our father once took Mother, Ryan, and me to a Thanksgiving parade.

   _____ Our Father once took mother, Ryan, and me to a thanksgiving parade.

5. _____ Mayor Frank McGinity wore an orange derby in the parade that thursday.

   ___C___ Mayor Frank McGinity wore an orange derby in the parade that Thursday.

**At Home:** Write a sentence that tells how your family celebrates your favorite holiday.

McGraw-Hill Language Arts
Grade 4, Unit 2, Nouns,
pages 98–99

5

---

## Mixed Review

**RULES**

- A **singular noun** names only one person, place, or thing.

  person → thing → place

  *A friend of mine formed a club in my neighborhood.*

- A **plural noun** names more than one person, place, or thing. Add **-s** to form the plural of most nouns.

  *My friends and I are interested in outer space.*

- Add **-es** to form the plural of nouns ending in *s, x, ch,* or *sh.*

  speech + es = speeches          class + es = classes

- To form the plural of nouns ending with a consonant and *y,* change the *y* to *i* and add **-es.**   family − y + i + es = families

- A **proper noun** is a noun that names a particular person, place, or thing. A proper noun always begins with a capital letter.

  **common nouns:** teacher     city
  **proper nouns:** Mr. Jarvis     Houston

A. Circle the correct form of the plural noun in parentheses.

1. We have been studying the (galaxys, (galaxies)).

2. Several (country, (countries)) want to work together to study outer space.

3. There are many (branchs, (branches)) of space science.

4. In some (citys, (cities)) there are huge telescopes to look at the stars.

5. Some ((friends), friendes) in my neighborhood formed a star club.

B. Write the proper noun(s) in each sentence and capitalize them.

1. We have been studying the galaxies.

2. Several countries want to work together to study outer space.     _____

3. There are many branches of space science.

4. In some cities there are huge telescopes to look at the stars.

5. Some friends in my neighborhood formed a star club.

6. Mrs. dunne teaches us about space.     **Mrs. Dunne**

7. She told us about a huge telescope in california.     **California**

8. It is at the palomar observatory.     **Palomar Observatory**

9. The telescope was designed by george hale.     **George Hale**

10. He was an american astronomer.     **American**

**At Home:** Look at the night sky with a family member. Write five sentence about what you see. Include some singular, plural, and proper nouns. Circle all the nouns you use.

10

McGraw-Hill Language Arts
Grade 4, Unit 2, Mixed Review,
pages 100–101

McGraw-Hill School Division

## Singular Possessive Nouns

**┌─ RULES ─┐**

- A **singular possessive noun** is a word that shows that something belongs to one person or thing.

  the **cell's** shape (the shape belongs to one cell)

  the **plant's** leaves (the leaves belong to one plant)

- Usually, make a singular noun possessive by adding an **apostrophe** with the letter **s** to a singular noun.

  The fur of an animal is made up of cells.

  An **animal's** fur is made up of cells.

  animal + 's = animal's

Rewrite each sentence using a singular possessive noun to replace some of the words in each underlined phrase.

Nucleus

Cell membrane

Cytoplasm

1. The cells of the body breathe, take in food, and eliminate wastes.
   **The body's cells breathe, take in food, and eliminate wastes.**

2. The nucleus in the center of a cell is the control point of the cell.
   **The nucleus in the center of a cell is the cell's control point.**

3. A purpose of the cell membrane is to hold the cell together.
   **A cell membrane's purpose is to hold the cell together.**

4. You can see cells using the microscope of the school.
   **You can see cells using the school's microscope.**

5. The nervous system of the body is made up of branched nerve cells.
   **The body's nervous system is made up of branched nerve cells.**

**At Home:** Write sentences telling about three items owned by different members of your family.

McGraw-Hill Language Arts
Grade 4, Unit 2, Nouns,
pages 102–103

5

---

## Plural Possessive Nouns

**┌─ RULES ─┐**

- A **plural possessive noun** is a word that shows something belongs to two or more persons or things.

  the **officials' plans** (the plans belong to more than one official)

- When a plural noun ends in s, add an **apostrophe** (') to form the plural possessive noun. If the plural noun does not end in **-s**, add an **apostrophe** and **-s ('s)**.

  the **brothers' baseball gloves**    **women's sports**

Write the letter **C** next to the phrase that has the same meaning as the underlined words in the sentence.

1. Groups of students will do volunteer work.
   - **C** ____ groups' students
   - ____ students' groups

2. The purposes of the groups will be to improve our community.
   - **C** ____ groups' purposes
   - ____ group's purposes

3. The reasons of my friends for volunteering are admirable.
   - **C** ____ my friends' reasons
   - ____ my friend's reasons

4. Some of the reasons of other children are different.
   - **C** ____ other children's reasons
   - ____ other childrens' reasons

5. All the members of the clubs are anxious to begin their projects.
   - ____ members' clubs
   - **C** ____ clubs' members

6. Some students will need the permission of both parents.
   - **C** ____ both parents' permission
   - ____ both parent's permission

7. Work will be done under the supervision of teachers.
   - ____ teacher's supervision
   - **C** ____ teachers' supervision

8. The principal requested cooperation of people at school.
   - **C** ____ people's cooperation
   - ____ cooperation's people

9. Many citizens of the neighborhoods will benefit from our work.
   - **C** ____ neighborhoods' citizens
   - ____ neighborhood's citizens

10. They will enjoy the benefits of the improvements.
    - ____ benefits' improvements
    - **C** ____ improvements' benefits

**At Home:** Rewrite five of the above sentences using the correct plural possessive noun.

McGraw-Hill Language Arts
Grade 4, Unit 2, Nouns,
pages 104–105

10

## Combining Sentences: Nouns

### RULES

- You can combine sentences that have similar ideas by joining two nouns with the conjunctions *and* or *or*.

**Combine nouns in the subject:**

*Andrea works at the library.* ⟍
*James works at the library.* ⟋  →  ***Andrea and James* work at the library.**

**Combine nouns in the predicate:**

*You can borrow books.* ⟍
*You can borrow tapes.* ⟋  →  *You can borrow **books or tapes**.*

Combine each pair of sentences using the word in parentheses.

1. Do you want to borrow books? Do you want to borrow periodicals? (or)

   Do you want to borrow books or periodicals?

2. Librarians are helpful for finding information. Card catalogs are helpful for finding information. (and)

   Librarians and card catalogs are helpful for finding information.

3. Library catalogs can be found on cards. Library catalogs can be found on computers. (or)

   Library catalogs can be found on cards or computers.

4. The card catalog lists hardbound books. The card catalog lists paperback books. (and)

   The card catalog lists hardbound books and paperback books.

5. Is your research for work? Is your research for school? (or)

   Is your research for work or school?

At Home: Underline the nouns that can be combined in each pair of sentences above.

McGraw-Hill Language Arts
Grade 4, Unit 2, Nouns,
pages 106–107

5

27

---

## Mechanics and Usage: Abbreviations

### RULES

- Most titles of people, days of the week, and months of the year can be made into a shorter form called an **abbreviation**.
- Begin abbreviations with a **capital letter**.
- End abbreviations with a **period**.

**Titles**

Mr. → Mister
Dr. → Doctor
Sen. → Senator
Gov. → Governor

**Days**

Mon. → Monday
Wed. → Wednesday
Thurs. → Thursday
Sun. → Sunday

**Months**

Jan. → January
Mar. → March
Sept. → September
Nov. → November

Circle the correct abbreviation for the underlined word and rewrite the phrase on the line.

1. a <u>Saturday</u> book club

   a Sat. book club          Satur.      S.D.      (Sat.)

2. <u>Mister</u> and Mrs. King

   Mr. and Mrs. King          (Mr.)      Miss      Msr.

3. meeting in <u>January</u>

   meeting in Jan.          Ja.      Jun.      (Jan.)

4. lecture by <u>Doctor</u> Bond

   lecture by Dr. Bond          Drs.      Doc.      (Dr.)

5. program about <u>Senator</u> McCord

   program about Sen. McCord          Str.      Sentr.      (Sen.)

At Home: Write all the days of the week and their abbreviations in the order they appear on the calendar.

McGraw-Hill Language Arts
Grade 4, Unit 2, Nouns,
pages 108–109

5

28

# Mixed Review

Name _____ Date _____

Reteach **29**

**RULES**

- To make a singular noun possessive, add an **apostrophe** and **-s.**
  theater + ' + s = *theater's*    *actors* + ' = *actors'*
- To make a plural noun that ends in s possessive, add an **apostrophe.**
- To make a plural noun that does not end in s possessive, add an **apostrophe** and **-s.**
  women + ' + s = *women's*
- You can **combine sentences** by joining two nouns with *and* or *or.*
  The theater had one floor. The theater had a balcony.
  *The theater had one floor and a balcony.*

**A.** Write the correct possessive form of each noun in parentheses.

1. (men) The _____ **men's** chorus is very talented.
2. (magician) The _____ **magician's** show is very clever.
3. (children) The _____ **children's** acts are very cute.
4. (dancers) The _____ **dancers'** costumes are very colorful.
5. (singer) The _____ **singer's** song was very beautiful.

**B.** Join two nouns with *and* or *or* to combine each pair of sentences.

6. I bought tickets. I bought programs.
   I bought tickets and programs.
7. The costumes were very imaginative. The sets were very imaginative.
   The costumes and sets were very imaginative.
8. The theater had new seats. The theater had new lounges.
   The theater had new seats and lounges.
9. The snack bar served sandwiches. The snack bar served drinks.
   The snack bar served sandwiches and drinks.
10. The musicians were great. The actors were great.
    The musicians and actors were great.

**At Home:** Write five sentences about a place you and your family have been. Include possessive nouns. Combine sentences when you can.

McGraw-Hill Language Arts
Grade 4, Unit 2, Mixed Review,
pages 110–111

29

10

---

# Common Errors: Plurals and Possessives

Name _____ Date _____

Reteach **30**

**RULES**

- A **plural noun** names more than one person, place, or thing. Most plural nouns are formed by adding **-s** or **-es.**
  lambs      foxes
- A **possessive noun** shows who or what owns or has something.
- A **singular possessive noun** is formed by adding **-'s.**
  cat + 's      cat's   whiskers
- A **plural possessive noun** that ends in **-s** is formed by adding **'.**
  dogs + '      dogs'  paws
- A **plural possessive noun** that does not end in **-s** is formed by adding **-'s.**
  mice + 's      mice's   tails

Write the possessive form of each underlined noun.

1. the zoo for <u>children</u>          **children's** zoo
2. the skin of a <u>snake</u>          **snake's** skin
3. the fur of <u>foxes</u>          **foxes'** fur
4. the feathers of <u>geese</u>          **geese's** feathers
5. the horns of a <u>goat</u>          **goat's** horns
6. the claws of an <u>eagle</u>          **eagle's** claws
7. the tails of <u>monkeys</u>          **monkeys'** tails
8. the spines on <u>hedgehogs</u>          **hedgehogs'** spines
9. the hooves on a <u>pony</u>          **pony's** hooves
10. the beaks on <u>parrots</u>          **parrots'** beaks

**At Home:** Write three sentences describing your favorite kind of animal. Include a possessive noun in each sentence.

McGraw-Hill Language Arts
Grade 4, Unit 2, Nouns,
pages 112–113

30

10

McGraw-Hill School Division

T15

## Study Skills: Parts of a Book

Certain parts of a book help you find information quickly.

In the front of a book you may find:

- a **title page** with the title, author, and the publisher of the book.
- a **copyright page** with the date the book was published.
- a **table of contents** listing the titles of chapters and the page numbers on which they begin.

In the back of a book you may find:

- a **glossary** with the spelling, pronunciation, and definition of important words in the book.
- an **index** with an alphabetical listing of all the topics in the book and the page numbers on which they can be found.

Look at the pages from a nonfiction book. On the line below each page, identify whether the page is a *title page*, *copyright page*, *table of contents*, *glossary*, or *index*.

**Z**

**zygote** (zī′ gōt)
Developing individual
produced from germ
cells.

1. _____ **glossary**

```
                    © 2001
           All rights reserved.
     Elsa Saldor Publishers, Inc.
           100 Union Square
      New York, New York 10000
      Printed in the United States of
                 America
       ISBN 0-01—000034-1/2
```

4. _____ **copyright page**

```
          All About the Cell
            by D. Ortega

      Elsa Saldor Publishers, Inc.
      San Diego • Chicago •
             New York
```

2. _____ **title page**

```
Microscope, 53
Mitochondria, 5, 89–91
Mitosis,
     definition, 27
     phases of cell division
              40–42
Molecular Biology, 65
Nucleus, 4, 33, 78, 99
```

5. _____ **index**

3. _____ **table of contents**

31

---

McGraw-Hill School Division

## Vocabulary: Compound Words

- A compound word is a word made from two or more smaller words that are joined together.

**brain + storm = brainstorm     down + stairs = downstairs**

**A.** Underline the compound word or words in each sentence. Put a diagonal line (/) between the smaller words that make up the compound word.

1. I wear my backpack to school every day. _____ **back/pack**

2. I also carry my lunchbox to school. _____ **lunch/box**

3. When I go to a football game, I pack a sandwich and a thermos with a hot drink. _____ **foot/ball**

4. After school, I swap trading cards with my classmates. _____ **class/mates**

5. On Saturday afternoon, I usually visit Granny, who gives me homemade cookies. _____ **after/noon, home/made**

**B.** Choose words from the word box to complete each compound word in a sentence.

| row | sand | sea | some | star | summer |
|-----|------|-----|------|------|--------|

6. I love the **summer** _____ time when we can go to the beach.

7. I help my little brother build **sand** _____ castles.

8. We found a beautiful **star** _____ fish that had washed ashore.

9. We always collect **sea** _____ shells that we can paint.

10. Dad takes us fishing in a **row** _____ boat.

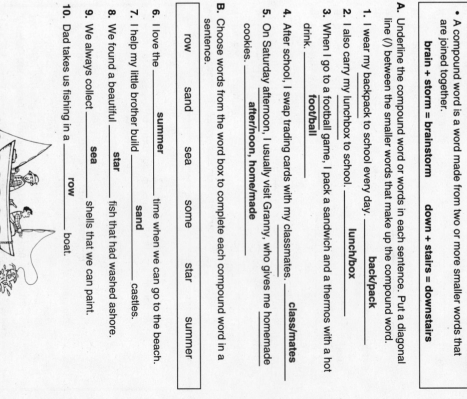

32

**At Home:** Choose words from the word box and make up other compound words. Read your list to a family member.

McGraw-Hill Language Arts
Grade 4, Unit 2, Vocabulary,
pages 122–123

10

## Composition: Writing Descriptions

- A good **description** is a vivid picture you create with words. Your word picture makes the reader feel like he or she knows the person, place, thing, or idea you are writing about.
- Put the pieces of the description together in logical order, such as from top to bottom or from side to side.
- In your description, include words and details that connect with a reader's sense of sight, smell, sound, taste, or touch.

| sense of sound | sense of smell |
|---|---|
| The siren hurt my ears. | The room smells like sweet vanilla. |

On the line, write the sense described in each sentence: *sight, smell, touch, taste, sound.* **Answers may vary.**

1. The baby squealed like a happy piglet. _____ **sound**

2. The sour candy made my lips pucker. _____ **taste**

3. Henry could sniff the smoke from the campfire. _____ **smell**

4. The palace blinded me with dazzling gold decorations. _____ **sight**

5. The wet sand felt like cool velvet. _____ **touch**

6. The train ahead of us groaned like a hurt animal. _____ **sound**

7. The bacon sizzled on the griddle. _____ **sound**

8. Blooming flowers filled the air with sweet perfume. _____ **smell**

9. The wind whipped my hair right to left across my cheeks. _____ **touch**

10. The scent of baking cookies lured us into the kitchen. _____ **smell**

At Home: What do your five senses tell you? Name each sense and tell how it helps you.

McGraw-Hill Language Arts
Grade 4, Unit 2, Composition Skills,
pages 124–125

☑ 10

---

## Action Verbs

### RULES

- An **action verb** is a verb that expresses action.
- An **action verb** tells what the subject does or did.

> Marsha *paints* pictures as a hobby.
> Marsha *draws* pictures as a hobby.
> Marsha *sketches* pictures as a hobby.

Write the action verb in each sentence.

1. Marsha taught herself how to paint. _____ **taught**

2. She read many books about painting. _____ **read**

3. She watched television shows about painting. _____ **watched**

4. She even talked to a few painters. _____ **talked**

5. Now Marsha paints whenever she can. _____ **paints**

6. She often makes sketches of animals. _____ **makes**

7. Sometimes she exhibits her paintings at art shows. _____ **exhibits**

8. She won several prizes for her work at the last show. _____ **won**

9. Several people commented on her paintings. _____ **commented**

10. She even sold two of her paintings to complete strangers. _____ **sold**

At Home: Write three sentences about something you like to do. Include an action verb in each sentence. Circle each action verb you write.

McGraw-Hill Language Arts
Grade 4, Unit 3, Verbs,
pages 170–171

☑ 10

## Verb Tenses

**RULES**

The tense of a verb tells you if something takes place in the present, in the past, or in the future.

• A verb in the **present tense** tells what happens now.
• A verb in the **past tense** tells what has already happened.
• A verb in the **future tense** tells what is going to happen.
  To write the future tense, use the special verb **will**.

| Present Tense | Past Tense | Future Tense |
|---|---|---|
| Insects survive almost everywhere. | They survived millions of years ago. | They will survive in the future. |

Circle whether the underlined verb is in the present, past, or future tense.

1. Our science teacher <u>decided</u> to teach about insects.
   present    (past)    future

2. She <u>told</u> us about the different kinds of insects.
   present    (past)    future

3. We <u>will spend</u> several days learning about them.
   present    past    (future)

4. The class <u>divides</u> into small groups.
   (present)    past    future

5. Each group <u>chooses</u> a kind of insect to study.
   (present)    past    future

6. At the end of the week, each group <u>will make</u> a presentation.
   present    past    (future)

7. The class <u>will take</u> a field trip to see a museum exhibit.
   present    past    (future)

8. The museum exhibit <u>shows</u> hundreds of kinds of insects.
   (present)    past    future

9. Everyone <u>voted</u> in favor of taking the trip.
   (present)    past    future

10. Afterward, the class <u>will discuss</u> what they saw.
    present    past    (future)

At Home: Write three sentences about a favorite topic. Write one sentence in the present tense, one in the past tense, and one in the future tense.

McGraw-Hill Language Arts
Grade 4, Unit 3, Verbs,
pages 172–173    ⬜/10

---

## Subject-Verb Agreement

**RULES**

• The subject and verb in a sentence must **agree**. If the subject is singular, the verb must be singular. If the subject is plural, the verb must be plural.

| Singular Subject | Plural Subject |
|---|---|
| Singular: he, she, or it | Plural: we, you, or they |
| To make most verbs singular, add -s. | Do not add -s or -es if the subject is plural or if it is I or you. |
| Add -es to verbs ending in s, ch, sh, x, or z. | |
| A **picture hangs** on my wall. | Several **pictures hang** on my wall. |

Write the correct form of the verb in parentheses.

1. Chen _____ **collects** _____ picture postcards. (collect)

2. He _____ **keeps** _____ his collection in special albums. (keep)

3. The cards _____ **remind** _____ him of places he has been. (remind)

4. He _____ **buys** _____ cards for his collection on family trips. (buy)

5. Most of the cards _____ **show** _____ scenes from the Southwest. (show)

6. Chen often _____ **visits** _____ there with his family. (visit)

7. Several cards _____ **include** _____ scenes of the Grand Canyon. (include)

8. Chen often _____ **wishes** _____ he could visit there again. (wish)

9. Sometimes people _____ **send** _____ Chen picture postcards. (send)

10. He _____ **adds** _____ them to his collection. (add)

⬜/10

At Home: Use a newspaper article to find two sentences with plural subjects and two sentences with singular subjects. Copy each sentence. Underline each subject. Circle each verb.

McGraw-Hill Language Arts
Grade 4, Unit 3, Verbs,
pages 174–175

McGraw-Hill School Division

T18

## Left page (Reteach 37)

# Spelling Present-Tense and Past-Tense Verbs

**RULES**

**Spelling Rules for Adding -es or -ed to Some Verbs**

- Change the *y* to *i* before adding -es or -ed to verbs that end with a consonant and *y*.

  *carry* = carries or carried

- Double the final consonant before adding -ed to one-syllable verbs that end with one vowel followed by one consonant.

  *trim* = trimmed

- Drop the *e* before adding -es or -ed to verbs that end in e.

  *smile* = smiles or smiled

Write the correct present-tense or past-tense form of each verb in parentheses.

1. Cody (shop) for a new camera. *present* — **shops**
2. Last week he (stop) at several stores. *past* — **stopped**
3. They all (carry) many kinds of cameras. *present* — **carry**
4. Cody (know) the special features of each kind. *present* — **knows**
5. He (remove) a camera from its case. *past* — **removed**
6. He (worry) that it was too large and heavy. *past* — **worried**
7. He (try) out another one with a zoom lens. *past* — **tried**
8. Cody (decide) to buy it. *past* — **decided**
9. He (hurry) home to try it out. *past* — **hurried**
10. That afternoon he (snap) pictures of everything. *past* — **snapped**

**At Home:** Look through a book you have read. Find five sentences with present-tense verbs. Find five sentences with past-tense verbs. List the verbs under the headings *Present Tense* and *Past Tense.*

McGraw-Hill Language Arts
Grade 4, Unit 3, Verbs,
pages 176–177

37 | 10

## Right page (Reteach 38)

# Mechanics and Usage: Commas in a Series

**RULES**

- A **comma** tells the reader to pause between the words that it separates.
- Use commas to separate items in a series of three or more words.
- Do not use a comma after the last word in a series.

  *Ted , Peter , Rosa , and Nora are neighbors.*

Rewrite each sentence. Use commas where they are needed.

1. Ted Peter Rosa and Nora made a garden together.
   **Ted, Peter, Rosa, and Nora made a garden together.**
2. They had to buy a rake a shovel and a hoe.
   **They had to buy a rake, a shovel, and a hoe.**
3. Rosa and Peter raked up rocks twigs and litter.
   **Rosa and Peter raked up rocks, twigs, and litter.**
4. Ted and Nora dug turned and raked the soil.
   **Ted and Nora dug, turned, and raked the soil.**
5. Together they decided to plant beans tomatoes carrots and corn.
   **Together they decided to plant beans, tomatoes, carrots, and corn.**
6. They planted petunias sunflowers and daisies along the edge.
   **They planted petunias, sunflowers, and daisies along the edge.**
7. Sun rain and care helped things grow quickly.
   **Sun, rain, and care helped things grow quickly.**
8. The friends took turns weeding hoeing and watering.
   **The friends took turns weeding, hoeing, and watering.**
9. Soon they were picking cooking and eating things from the garden.
   **Soon they were picking, cooking, and eating things from the garden.**
10. Making the garden was enjoyable successful and practical.
   **Making the garden was enjoyable, successful, and practical.**

**At Home:** Write about something you have done with friends. Include at least three sentences that have a series of three or more words.

McGraw-Hill Language Arts
Grade 4, Unit 3, Verbs,
pages 178–179

38 | 10

# Mixed Review

## RULES

- Action verbs in the **present tense** tell what is happening now.
- Action verbs in the **past tense** tell what happened in the past.
- Action verbs in the **future tense** tell what will happen in the future.
- Add -s to most present-tense verbs if the subject is singular. Add -es to verbs that end in s, ch, sh, x, or z. Do not add -s or -es if the subject is plural or I or you.
- For verbs ending in a consonant and y, change the y to i before adding -es or -ed.
- For one-syllable verbs ending in one vowel and one consonant, double the consonant before adding -ed.
- For verbs ending in e, drop the e before adding -ed.

**A.** Circle the correct tense of the underlined verb.

1. My father learned to play the piano at an early age.    present (past) future
2. He enjoys playing the piano for friends.    (present) past future
3. Practice will make him even better than he is now.    present past (future)
4. I like to listen to guitar music on the radio.    (present) past future
5. Someday I will take guitar lessons.    present past (future)

**B.** Write the verb in parentheses ( ) that completes each sentence.

6. Two of my friends (play, plays) musical instruments.    __play__
7. Marta (take, takes) piano lessons every week.    __takes__
8. John (practice, practices) the saxophone.    __practices__
9. My parents (want, wants) me to learn how to play.    __want__
10. It (amaze, amazes) me when I see people playing music.    __amazes__

**At Home:** Find out if someone in your family plays a musical instrument. Write a paragraph about it. Include some verbs in the present, past, and future tense.

McGraw-Hill Language Arts
Grade 4, Unit 3, Mixed Review,
pages 180–181

| 10 |

---

# Main Verbs and Helping Verbs

## RULES

- The **main verb** is the most important verb in a sentence. It tells what the subject does or is.
  *The puppet show will **begin** in an hour.*
- A **helping verb** is a verb that comes before the main verb. It helps the main verb show an action or make a statement.
  *The puppet show **will** begin in an hour.*

| Helping Verbs |
|---|
| am, is, are, was, were, has, have, had, will |

Read each sentence. Write the helping verb in the first column and the main verb in the second column.

1. A theater group was performing a puppet show.    __was__    __performing__
2. The puppets were dressed in colorful costumes.    __were__    __dressed__
3. The puppet theater was designed like an ancient castle.    __was__    __designed__
4. The puppets are attached to strings.    __are__    __attached__
5. The puppeteers were standing above the puppet theater.    __were__    __standing__
6. They will work the strings to bring the puppets to life.    __will__    __work__
7. They are using a different voice for each character.    __are__    __using__
8. The children are watching in amazement.    __are__    __watching__
9. Even the adults were enjoying themselves.    __were__    __enjoying__
10. The puppets had won everyone's admiration.    __had__    __won__

**At Home:** Write three sentences about something interesting you have watched. Include a helping verb and a main verb in each sentence.

McGraw-Hill Language Arts
Grade 4, Unit 3, Verbs,
pages 182–183

| 10 |

## Using Helping Verbs

**RULES**

- *Has*, *have*, and *had* are helping verbs. You can use them with the past-tense form of a verb to show an action that has already happened.

Use *has* with a singular subject and *he, she, or it*.

> My sister *has sailed* on a boat.
> She *has sailed* many times.

Use *have* with plural subjects and *I, you, we, or they*.

> Many people *have sailed* on the ocean.
> I *have sailed* on the lake.

Use *had* with singular or plural subjects.

> My friend *had sailed* last summer.
> My friends *had sailed* at camp.

Write the correct form of the helping verb in parentheses.

1. Whale watching __**has**__ attracted many tourists. (have, has)

2. Many people __**have**__ enjoyed the thrill of seeing whales. (have, has)

3. My friends and I __**have**__ decided to go whale watching. (have, has)

4. The boat __**had**__ sailed several times that day. (have, had)

5. On the first trip, the passengers __**had**__ spotted many whales. (has, had)

6. The whales __**have**__ discovered a good feeding area. (have, has)

7. The boat's captain __**had**__ sighted them not far away. (have, had)

8. One whale __**has**__ surfaced beside the boat. (have, has)

9. A few whales __**had**__ leaped into the air. (has, had)

10. Now they __**have**__ crashed back into the water. (have, has)

McGraw-Hill Language Arts
Grade 4, Unit 3, Verbs,
pages 184–185

**At Home:** Find a picture in a magazine that you like. Write three sentences about it. Use the helping verbs *have, has,* or *had* in each sentence.

**10**

---

## Linking Verbs

**RULES**

- An **action verb** tells what the subject does or did.

> *Nocturnal animals **sleep** during the day.*

- A **linking verb** links the subject of a sentence to a noun or adjective in the predicate. A linking verb does not express action.

> *Nocturnal animals **are** creatures of the night.*

- The words *am, is, are, was,* and *were* are important linking verbs. They are forms of the verb *be.*

Tell whether each underlined verb is an action verb or a linking verb. Write your answer.

1. Nocturnal animals <u>are</u> nighttime creatures. __linking verb__

2. They <u>sleep</u> during most of the day. __action verb__

3. Bats <u>are</u> nocturnal animals. __linking verb__

4. They <u>live</u> in caves during the day. __action verb__

5. They <u>hunt</u> for food during the night. __action verb__

6. Bats <u>are</u> the only mammals that can fly. __linking verb__

7. There <u>are</u> more than 900 kinds of bats. __linking verb__

8. I <u>am</u> one of their greatest fans. __linking verb__

9. Once I <u>was</u> at the entrance to a bat cave. __linking verb__

10. At dusk, the bats <u>flew</u> out of the cave. __action verb__

11. It <u>was</u> a terrific and awesome sight. __linking verb__

12. One large bat <u>is</u> the flying fox. __linking verb__

13. It <u>makes</u> its home in tropical forests. __action verb__

14. Brown bats <u>are</u> much smaller. __linking verb__

15. They <u>inhabit</u> many parts of the United States. __action verb__

McGraw-Hill Language Arts
Grade 4, Unit 3, Verbs,
pages 186–187

**At Home:** Read a paragraph from a magazine or newspaper article to a family member. Identify any linking verbs you see.

**15**

## Page 43

# Using Linking Verbs

## RULES

- **Am, is,** and **are** are **present-tense linking verbs.** They must agree with the subject of the sentence. Subjects can be singular or plural.

  **Singular:** *I, he, she, it*    **Plural:** *you, we, they*

  She **is** a musician. *(singular)*    You **are** musicians. *(plural)*

- **Was** and **were** are **past-tense linking verbs.** They must agree with the subject of the sentence. Subjects can be singular or plural.

  She **was** a musician. *(singular)*    They **were** musicians. *(plural)*

Rewrite the sentence with the correct form of the linking verb in parentheses.

1. Anita (is, are) a member of the orchestra.
   Anita is a member of the orchestra.

2. Orchestras (is, are) large groups of musicians.
   Orchestras are large groups of musicians.

3. Anita (is, were) one of the violin players.
   Anita is one of the violin players.

4. I (am, were) one of the cellists.
   I am one of the cellists.

5. Last year our concerts (was, were) very popular.
   Last year our concerts were very popular.

6. Our conductor (was, were) Mr. Ortez.
   Our conductor was Mr. Ortez.

7. All of our musicians (is, are) first rate.
   All of our musicians are first rate.

8. They (are, was) wonderful when they play together.
   They are wonderful when they play together.

9. Everyone (is, were) very proud to be a member.
   Everyone is very proud to be a member.

10. Our first concert this year (was, were) a huge success.
    Our first concert this year was a huge success.

**At Home:** Write three sentences about music. Use linking verbs in each sentence.

McGraw-Hill Language Arts
Grade 4, Unit 3, Verbs,
pages 188–189

43    10

---

## Page 44

# Irregular Verbs

## RULES

- You do not always add **-ed** to form the past tense of verbs. Verbs that do not add **-ed** to form the past tense are called **irregular verbs.**

- Most irregular verbs change their spelling to form the past tense.

  Here are some examples.

| Verb | Past | Past with has, have, or had |
|------|------|------------------------------|
| go | went | gone |
| do | did | done |
| see | saw | seen |
| run | ran | run |
| come | came | come |
| give | gave | given |
| sing | sang | sung |
| eat | ate | eaten |
| make | made | made |
| bring | brought | brought |

Write the correct past tense form of the verb in parentheses.

1. Rosa and Luis had (go) ___gone___ to the wild animal park.

2. They have (see) ___seen___ some of the exhibits before.

3. Some of the animals (come) ___came___ out to play.

4. Monkeys (run) ___ran___ through an artificial rain forest.

5. The large cats (give) ___gave___ a roaring performance.

6. The elephants (make) ___made___ loud trumpeting sounds.

7. Rosa and Luis had (bring) ___brought___ a picnic lunch with them.

8. They (eat) ___ate___ it near the tropical bird exhibit.

9. Some of the birds (sing) ___sang___ unfamiliar songs.

10. Rosa and Luis had (do) ___done___ this before.

**At Home:** Write about something you have done with friends. Include at least three sentences that use irregular verbs in the past tense.

McGraw-Hill Language Arts
Grade 4, Unit 3, Verbs,
pages 190–191

44    10

## More Irregular Verbs

**RULES**
- **Irregular** verbs do not add **-ed** to form the past tense. Instead, the spelling of an irregular verb changes.

| Verb | Past | Past with has, have, or had |
|---|---|---|
| begin | began | begun |
| draw | drew | drawn |
| drive | drove | driven |
| fly | flew | flown |
| grow | grew | grown |
| ride | rode | ridden |
| swim | swam | swum |
| take | took | taken |
| throw | threw | thrown |
| write | wrote | written |

Circle the correct form of the verb in parentheses.

1. My family has (did, **done**) many interesting things.
2. My brother (fly, **flew**) in a helicopter.
3. My sister has (swam, **swum**) in many swimming meets.
4. I have (rode, **ridden**) in bicycle marathons.
5. My mom has (drew, **drawn**) pictures of us.
6. My dad (**began**, begun) to take flying lessons.
7. My grandfather has (**driven**, drove) race cars.
8. My grandmother (**wrote**, written) a book.
9. My parents have (took, **taken**) dancing lessons.
10. My uncle has (grew, **grown**) prize-winning roses.

**At Home:** Write three sentences about something you used to do when you were younger. Use an irregular verb in each sentence.

45

McGraw-Hill Language Arts
Grade 4, Unit 3, Verbs,
pages 192–193

10

---

## Mechanics and Usage: Contractions with *Not*

**RULES**
- A **contraction** is a shortened form of two words. An **apostrophe** (') takes the place of one or more letters that are left out. Several contractions are made by combining a verb and the word *not*.

**does + not = does + n't = doesn't**

| is not | isn't | has not | hasn't |
|---|---|---|---|
| are not | aren't | have not | haven't |
| was not | wasn't | had not | hadn't |
| were not | weren't | do not | don't |
| will not | won't | did not | didn't |

**A.** Draw lines to match the contractions and the words.

1. was not — aren't
2. has not — isn't
3. do not — wasn't
4. will not — won't
5. have not — doesn't
6. does not — hasn't
7. is not — haven't
8. did not — weren't
9. are not — didn't
10. were not — don't

**B.** Write the two words that make up each contraction in parentheses.

11. I (haven't) **have not** seen a purple sky.
12. I (don't) **do not** have green hair.
13. Trees (aren't) **are not** blue and gold.
14. A car (doesn't) **does not** talk to you.
15. I (won't) **will not** ever see a cow that flies.

**At Home:** Read an article in a newspaper or magazine. Make a list of all the contractions you find.

46

McGraw-Hill Language Arts
Grade 4, Unit 3, Verbs,
pages 194–195

15

McGraw-Hill School Division

T23

## Mixed Review

**RULES**

- The **main verb** in a sentence shows what a subject does or is. It is the most important verb.

  *I **acted** in the class play.*

- A **helping verb** comes before the main verb. It helps the main verb show an action or make a statement.

  *I had **learned** my lines well.*

  | Helping Verbs |
  |---|
  | am, is, are, was, were, has, have, had, will |

- A **linking verb** links the subject of a sentence to a noun or adjective in the predicate. A linking verb does not express action.

  *The play **was** a great success.*

  | Linking Verbs |
  |---|
  | am, is, are, was, were |

Draw one line under each main verb. Draw two lines under each helping verb. Circle each linking verb.

1. I (am) a member of the class play.

2. Many of my friends (are) in the play, too.

3. We <u>have</u> <u>written</u> our own play to perform.

4. My friend Jill (is) the lead character.

5. She <u>has</u> <u>learned</u> all her lines well.

6. The cast <u>has</u> <u>rehearsed</u> many times.

7. Our teacher <u>has</u> <u>helped</u> us every night.

8. She thinks we <u>are</u> <u>doing</u> a great job.

9. The costumes and props <u>will</u> <u>surprise</u> everyone.

10. Putting on a play (is) a hard job.

At Home: Write a paragraph about a movie or television show you have watched. Use main, helping, and linking verbs.

McGraw-Hill Language Arts
Grade 4, Unit 3, Mixed Review,
pages 196–197

10

---

## Common Errors: Subject-Verb Agreement

**RULES**

- When parts of a compound subject are joined by **and**, use a **plural verb**.

  *Juan and Mario **play** trumpets.*

- When the parts of a compound subject are joined by **or**, the verb agrees with the subject that is closer to it.

  *Songs or a dance **begins** the show.*

  *Either a table or trays **hold** snacks.*

- When a verb ends with a consonant and **y**, add **-es** to form a singular verb. *fly → flies*

- When a verb ends with a vowel and **y**, add **-s** to form a singular verb. Do not change the spelling of the verb. *spray → sprays*

Complete each sentence. Write the verb in parentheses ( ) that agrees with the compound subject of each sentence.

1. The music class or art club ____ **is** ____ having a talent show. (is, are)

2. The girls and boys ____ **present** ____ variety acts. (presents, present)

3. Linda and Kelly ____ **sing** ____ a duet. (sings, sing)

4. My sister and brother ____ **perform** ____ bicycle tricks. (performs, perform)

5. Either Mark or Shelly ____ **does** ____ magic tricks. (do, does)

6. Either my teacher or her husband ____ **plays** ____ the guitar. (plays, play)

7. Taki and Miko ____ **play** ____ together on the piano. (plays, play)

8. My family and friends ____ **sit** ____ in the audience. (sits, sit)

9. Cheers or applause ____ **comes** ____ from everywhere. (comes, come)

10. Both performers and audience ____ **enjoy** ____ the show. (enjoys, enjoy)

At Home: Write three sentences about the talents you or family members have. Include compound subjects in each sentence.

McGraw-Hill Language Arts
Grade 4, Unit 3, Verbs,
pages 198–199

10

## Study Skills: Card Catalog

- Use the alphabetically arranged **card catalog** to locate a book in the library. You will find it in a set of drawers or on a computer.
- Look at the **author cards, title cards,** or **subject cards** in the card catalog. Each kind of card gives the same information in a different order.
- Use the **call number** on the upper-left part of the card. Each kind of card for the same book shows the same call number.

> 629.8
> D
>
> D'Ignazio, Fred
> Working Robots.
> New York: Lodestar Books, © 1982.
> 149 p.: illus.

The **author card** lists the author's last name first.

The **title card** shows the title first.

> 629.45
> M
>
> Animals in Orbit.
> McGlade Marko, Katherine
> New York: Franklin Watts, © 1991.
> 61 p.: illus.

The **subject card** begins with the subject of the book.

> 629.44    SPACE
> C
>
> Cross, Wilbur and Susanna
> Space Shuttle.
> Chicago: Children's Press, © 1988.
> 134 p.: illus.

Use the sample catalog cards above to answer each question.

1. What is the title of the book about space? _____ **Space Shuttle**

2. Who wrote the book *Animals in Orbit?* _____ **Katherine McGlade Marko**

3. In what year was the book *Animals in Orbit* published? _____ **1991**

4. How many of the books have illustrations? _____ **all of them**

5. Which of the three books has the most pages? _____ **Working Robots**

6. Which book has a title card on this page? _____ **Animals in Orbit**

7. What is the call number of the book about the space shuttle? _____ **629.44 C**

8. In what year was the book *Working Robots* published? _____ **1982**

9. Which book was published in Chicago? _____ **Space Shuttle**

10. Who is the author of the book about robots? _____ **Fred D'Ignazio**

**At Home:** Think about a subject that interests you. Then make up the information for a book on this subject and write a subject card for it.

McGraw-Hill Language Arts
Grade 4, Unit 3, Study Skills,
pages 206–207 [10]

---

## Vocabulary: Prefixes

- A **prefix** is a word part added to the beginning of a word. A prefix changes the meaning of the base word.
- A **base word** is a word to which a prefix is added.
  **in** + **complete**     **dis** + **obey**     **im** + **perfect**
- You can figure out the meaning of a word by putting together the meaning of the prefix with the meaning of the base word.

| Prefix | Meaning |
|--------|---------|
| dis | not, opposite of |
| im | not, opposite of |
| in | not without |
| mis | wrongly or opposite of |
| non | not |
| re | again |

Choose a word from the word box that completes each sentence. Write it on the line. Then circle the prefix of the word you write.

| uncomfortable | multiscreen | impossible | dislike | previews |
| impatient | unreal | recount | misunderstand | disbelief |

1. I go to movies at a (**multi**)screen _____ theater.

2. I like to watch movie (**pre**)views _____ .

3. Sometimes I am (**im**)patient _____ with the action.

4. That's when I (**re**)count _____ the story to my friends.

5. Some movies make me feel (**un**)comfortable _____ .

6. I (**dis**)like _____ lots of gooey romantic stuff.

7. Special effects can show things that are (**im**)possible _____ .

8. My sister doesn't like movies that are (**un**)real _____ .

9. I just listen to her in (**dis**)belief _____ .

10. Maybe I just (**mis**)understand _____ her.

**At Home:** In a dictionary, look up each prefix you circled and write its definition.

McGraw-Hill Language Arts
Grade 4, Unit 3, Vocabulary,
pages 208–209 [10]

## Composition Skills: Leads and Endings

- The first sentence in a persuasive composition is the **lead.** It should capture the attention of your reader.

  *I remember when I first met Max.*

- The last sentence is the **ending.** To help your reader feel that your writing is complete, end by drawing a conclusion, summarizing the main idea, or restating it.

  *Now I believe in happy endings.*

Circle the word *lead* or *ending* for each sentence.

1. The book sale you've been waiting for will take place next week.

   (lead)    ending

2. So, I ask for your vote as student representative for our class.

   lead    (ending)

3. You'll never regret hiring Darla as your pet sitter.

   lead    (ending)

4. Why do students want to be volunteers?

   (lead)    ending

5. Never forget that recycling protects the environment.

   lead    (ending)

6. Would you like to run faster and feel healthier?

   (lead)    ending

7. Some students in our school will start a math tutoring service.

   (lead)    ending

8. Now you know that bicycle riders with helmets are also smart riders.

   lead    (ending)

9. Have you signed up for an after-school activity yet?

   (lead)    ending

10. Talented students are available as tutors in a new student tutoring program.

    (lead)    ending

**At Home:** Pick a lead or ending that you like from the exercise above. For a lead, write an appropriate ending. For an ending, write an appropriate lead.

51

---

## Adjectives

**RULES**

**Adjectives** are words that describe nouns. can tell **what kind** and **how many.** usually come before the nouns they describe.

*Elephants are large animals.    There are two kinds of elephants.*

*There are African elephants.    There are Indian elephants.*

Circle the adjective in each sentence. Write the noun that the adjective describes.

1. Elephants are (strong) animals. _____ animals

2. They are also (intelligent) animals. _____ animals

3. The trunk of an elephant is a (remarkable) feature. _____ feature

4. It can be used for (many) purposes. _____ purposes

5. The trunk can be used to drink or spray (cool) water. _____ water

6. It can be used to pick up a (small) nut. _____ nut

7. It can also be used to rip up a (huge) tree. _____ tree

8. Elephants can be trained to be (excellent) helpers. _____ helpers

9. They can easily move (heavy) objects. _____ objects

10. They can carry people on their (strong) backs. _____ backs

11. Elephants live together in (large) groups. _____ groups

12. They can live for (many) years. _____ years

13. People used to hunt elephants for (ivory) tusks. _____ tusks

14. The (beautiful) tusks were used to make things. _____ tusks

15. Today, (strict) laws protect elephants from hunters. _____ laws

**At Home:** Write a description about something or someone. Include as many adjectives as you can.

52

## Articles: a, an, the

### RULES

The words **a**, **an**, and **the** are special adjectives called **articles**.

- Use **a** and **an** before singular nouns. Use **a** if the next word begins with a consonant sound. Use **an** if the next word begins with a vowel sound.

  *A lynx is **an** animal.*

- Use **the** before a singular noun that names a particular person, place, or thing.

  *The lynx is a kind of wild cat.*

- Use **the** before plural nouns.

  *The mountains are home to some wildcats.*

Choose the correct article in parentheses to complete each sentence. Write it on the line.

1. __An__ elephant may use its trunk to pet her baby. (A, An)

2. __The__ ostrich uses its long, powerful toes for defense. (The, A)

3. Stripes on __a__ zebra help it hide from its enemies. (a, an)

4. __An__ anteater really eats ants. (A, An)

5. At birth, __a__ giraffe is about six feet tall. (a, an)

6. Cheetahs are __the__ animals that can run the fastest. (an, the)

7. The tongue of __a__ chameleon is as long as its body. (a, an)

8. __The__ bee hummingbird is the smallest of all birds. (An, The)

9. __A__ coconut crab can climb trees. (A, An)

10. __An__ eagle's eyes are made so that it can see from great distances. (A, An)

At Home: Write five adjectives about your favorite animal. Include at least one article in each sentence.

McGraw-Hill Language Arts
Grade 4, Unit 4, Adjectives,
pages 264–265

10

---

## Adjectives After Linking Verbs

### RULES

- An **adjective** is a word that describes a noun.
- Sometimes an adjective **follows** the noun it describes.
- When an adjective follows the noun it describes, the noun and adjective are connected by a **linking verb**.
- The **linking verb** is usually a form of the verb be.

  *Summer **is** wonderful.*    *The days **are** long.*
  *The temperature **was** high.*    *The days **were** sunny.*

Circle each linking verb. Then write the adjective that describes each underlined noun.

1. The <u>summer</u> (is) relaxing.     relaxing

2. The long <u>days</u> (are) warm.     warm

3. <u>Sports</u> in the summer (are) fun.     fun

4. <u>Swimming</u> in the lake (is) popular.     popular

5. Last <u>summer</u> (was) perfect for me.     perfect

6. Winter <u>days</u> (are) shorter.     shorter

7. Winter <u>weather</u> (is) colder.     colder

8. Last <u>winter</u> (was) snowy.     snowy

9. Many <u>days</u> (were) freezing.     freezing

10. Sometimes winter <u>days</u> (are) beautiful.     beautiful

At Home: Look for linking verbs followed by adjectives in a newspaper or magazine article.

McGraw-Hill Language Arts
Grade 4, Unit 4, Adjectives,
pages 266–267

10

McGraw-Hill School Division

## Mechanics and Usage: Proper Adjectives

┌─ **RULES** ─────────────────────────────────────────────┐

- **Proper adjectives** are formed from proper nouns. They refer to a particular person, place, or thing.
- **Proper adjectives** are always capitalized.

| | |
|---|---|
| Europe ⟶ | **European** |
| North America ⟶ | **North American** |

*European* explorers

*North American* coast

└────────────────────────────────────────────────────────┘

Underline each proper adjective. Then write the noun it describes.

1. Have you read about <u>American</u> history? _____ history

2. Christopher Columbus was an <u>Italian</u> citizen. _____ citizen

3. He sailed to America for a <u>Spanish</u> queen. _____ queen

4. Columbus landed on a <u>Caribbean</u> island. _____ island

5. He never landed on the <u>North American</u> mainland. _____ mainland

6. A <u>German</u> mapmaker named the Americas. _____ mapmaker

7. <u>Spanish</u> explorers arrived in Mexico. _____ explorers

8. A <u>Portuguese</u> sailor landed in South America. _____ sailor

9. Many <u>Italian</u> explorers traveled to America. _____ explorers

10. John Cabot made the first <u>English</u> voyage to North America. _____ voyage

11. Jamestown was the first <u>British</u> settlement in North America. _____ settlement

12. Many <u>Spanish</u> missions were built in the west. _____ missions

13. The new world also saw the arrival of <u>French</u> traders. _____ traders

14. The early colonies were ruled by an <u>English</u> king. _____ king

15. People from other <u>European</u> countries also settled here. _____ countries

**At Home:** List the names of five countries you have heard of. Then write a sentence about each one. Include a proper adjective in each sentence.

**McGraw-Hill Language Arts** Grade 4, Unit 4, **Adjectives,** pages 268–269

☐/15

---

## Mixed Review

┌─ **RULES** ─────────────────────────────────────────────┐

- An **adjective** is a word that describes a noun. Adjectives tell *what kind* and *how many*. **red** *flower*   **old** *house*   **two** *teams*
- When an adjective comes after a noun it describes, the two are connected by a **linking verb.**

    *Summer is wonderful.*   *The temperatures are warm.*

- **Proper adjectives** are formed from proper nouns. **A proper adjective is** always capitalized.   *Europe → European*   *European countries*

└────────────────────────────────────────────────────────┘

A. Underline each adjective. Then write the noun it describes.

1. People have <u>interesting</u> hobbies. _____ hobbies

2. I knew someone that collected <u>ancient</u> coins. _____ coins

3. The coins are <u>valuable</u> because of their age. _____ coins

4. My grandfather makes <u>ship</u> models. _____ models

5. He keeps the models in <u>display</u> cases. _____ cases

6. He has at least <u>seven</u> models on display. _____ models

7. My grandmother collects and dries <u>wild</u> flowers. _____ flowers

8. She arranges them in <u>glass</u> vases. _____ vases

9. I like to make <u>miniature</u> models. _____ models

10. I have <u>twelve</u> airplanes hanging in my room. _____ airplanes

B. Write each proper adjective correctly. Circle the noun it describes.

11. I saw a collection of native american (art) at the museum. _____ Native American

12. There is a collection of asian (art) at the museum. _____ Asian

13. I have a book about the egyptian (pyramids). _____ Egyptian

14. My brother wrote an article about mexican (carvings). _____ Mexican

15. The museum has some examples of roman (sculpture). _____ Roman

**At Home:** Do you or a member of your family collect something? Write a paragraph about the collection. Then underline each adjective you used and circle the noun it describes.

**McGraw-Hill Language Arts** Grade 4, Unit 4, **Mixed Review,** pages 270–271

☐/15

## Adjectives That Compare

Name _____ Date _____ **Reteach 57**

**RULES**

- Adjectives that compare nouns often end in -*er* or -*est*.
- An adjective + -*er* compares two people, places, or things.

  *Cats are **faster** than dogs.*

- An adjective + -*est* compares more than two people, places, or things.

  *Cheetahs are the **fastest** animals.*

Write the correct form of the adjective in parentheses.

1. Cats are usually (smaller, smallest) than dogs. _____ smaller
2. Cats are among the (cleaner, cleanest) animals of all. _____ cleanest
3. Cats have (sharper, sharpest) vision than humans. _____ sharper
4. Cats have (sharper, sharpest) claws than dogs. _____ sharper
5. Some cats are (quicker, quickest) eaters than others. _____ quicker
6. Persian cats have the (longer, longest) hair of all cats. _____ longest
7. Rex cats have the (shorter, shortest) hair of any cat. _____ shortest
8. Persian cats have (fuller, fullest) tails than Burmese cats. _____ fuller
9. Siamese cats are among the (louder, loudest) cats. _____ loudest
10. Angora cats are one of the (older, oldest) kinds of all cats. _____ oldest

Maine Coon

Siamese

Manx

Persian

**At Home:** Make a list of adjectives that compare. Try to use at least one of the adjectives each day until you have used them all.

McGraw-Hill Language Arts
Grade 4, Unit 4, Adjectives,
pages 272–273

57 / 10

---

## Spelling Adjectives That Compare

Name _____ Date _____ **Reteach 58**

**RULES**

When adding -*er* or -*est* to adjectives, follow these spelling rules:

- If an adjective ends with **e**, drop the **e**, then add -*er* or -*est*.

  *little* (drop the e): *littler  littlest*

- If an adjective ends with a consonant and a **y**, change the **y** to **i** and add -*er* or -*est*.

  *heavy* (change y to i): *heavier  heaviest*

- If an adjective has a single vowel before a final consonant, double the final consonant, then add -*er* or -*est*.

  *flat* (double final consonant): *flatter  flattest*

Write the correct -*er* or -*est* form of the adjective in parentheses ( ).

1. (hot) This summer is _____ hotter _____ than last summer.
2. (nice) My flower garden is _____ nicer _____ than last year's garden.
3. (pretty) The roses are _____ prettier _____ this year than last year.
4. (lovely) I think red roses are the _____ loveliest _____ of all the roses.
5. (large) My neighbor's vegetable garden is _____ larger _____ than mine.
6. (tasty) My tomatoes are _____ tastier _____ than my neighbor's tomatoes.
7. (tiny) Cherry tomatoes are _____ tinier _____ than plum tomatoes.
8. (heavy) I grew the _____ heaviest _____ squash in the neighborhood.
9. (huge) My uncle grew the _____ hugest _____ pumpkin I ever saw.
10. (happy) Gardeners are the _____ happiest _____ people you'll ever meet.

**At Home:** Write five sentences about something you like to do. Include at least one adjective that changes its spelling in each sentence.

McGraw-Hill Language Arts
Grade 4, Unit 4, Adjectives,
pages 274–275

58 / 10

McGraw-Hill School Division

**T29**

## Comparing with More and Most

**RULES**

- Use **more** or **most** with most longer adjectives. Use **more** to compare two people, places or things. Use **most** to compare more than two people, places, or things.

  I think plays are **more enjoyable** than movies.
  I think plays are the **most enjoyable** form of entertainment.

- Never use **more** or **most** with an adjective that already has an **-er** or **-est** ending.

Choose the word in parentheses that completes each sentence.

1. Our local theater is (more, most) impressive this year than last year. _____ **more**

2. This year's play is the (more, most) entertaining one we have put on. _____ **most**

3. The costumes are the (more, most) beautiful I have ever seen. _____ **most**

4. The stage sets are (more, most) elaborate than they were last year. _____ **more**

5. The actors are the (more, most) effective performers in this state. _____ **most**

6. Last night's performance was (more, most) enjoyable than yesterday's performance. _____ **more**

7. The performers seemed (more, most) relaxed than they were yesterday. _____ **more**

8. The leading character is the (more, most) interesting part of all. _____ **most**

9. The actress who plays the part is the (more, most) popular of all the performers. _____ **most**

10. She is the (more, most) prepared of anyone in the show. _____ **most**

**At Home:** Think of two television programs you like to watch. Write five sentences comparing them using *more* or *most*.

McGraw-Hill Language Arts
Grade 4, Unit 4, Adjectives,
pages 276–277

59 | 10

---

## Comparing with Good and Bad

**RULES**

- The adjectives **good** and **bad** have special forms when used to compare.
- Use **better** and **worse** to compare two people, places, or things.

  This summer was **better** than last summer.
  Last summer was **worse** than this summer.

- Use **best** or **worst** to compare more than two people, places, or things.

  This was the **best** summer I can remember.
  Last summer was the **worst** summer I can remember.

Write the correct form of the word in parentheses ( ) to complete each sentence.

1. This summer camp was _____ than the last one. (good) **better**

2. The lake was the _____ I ever swam in. (good) **best**

3. My swimming team was _____ than my friend's team. (bad) **worse**

4. The camp counselors were the _____ I've ever had. (good) **best**

5. The food was the _____ I ever tasted. (bad) **worst**

6. The crafts classes were _____ than the woodworking classes. (good) **better**

7. The soccer coaches were _____ than the baseball coaches. (bad) **worse**

8. Swimming was _____ than hiking. (good) **better**

9. The camp singing was the _____ I ever heard. (bad) **worst**

10. Hiking was _____ than bird watching. (good) **better**

**At Home:** Write five sentences comparing two summers you can remember. Use forms of good or bad in each sentence.

McGraw-Hill Language Arts
Grade 4, Unit 4, Adjectives,
pages 278–279

60 | 10

# Combining Sentences: Adjectives

**RULES**

You can sometimes combine sentences by writing the adjective from one sentence in the other. Leave out the words that are the same in both sentences.

*Rico saw some monkeys.* The monkeys were *playful.*

*Rico saw some playful monkeys.*

Write each pair of sentences as one sentence.

1. Rico visited a zoo. The zoo was interesting.

   **Rico visited an interesting zoo.**

2. He saw some lions. The lions were scary.

   **He saw some scary lions.**

3. He watched some elephants. The elephants were enormous.

   **He watched some enormous elephants.**

4. Rico watched the elephants being fed. The elephants were hungry.

   **Rico watched the hungry elephants being fed.**

5. After they ate, the elephants did some tricks. The tricks were clever.

   **After they ate, the elephants did some clever tricks.**

6. Rico visited the reptile exhibit. The exhibit was new.

   **Rico visited the new reptile exhibit.**

7. There were many kinds of snakes. The snakes were exotic.

   **There were many kinds of exotic snakes.**

8. There were also many lizards. The lizards were unusual.

   **There were also many unusual lizards.**

9. Then Rico went to see the birds. The birds were tropical.

   **Then Rico went to see the tropical birds.**

10. There were many kinds of parrots. The parrots were colorful.

    **There were many kinds of colorful parrots.**

At Home: Write three pairs of sentences about a place you have visited. Then combine each pair into one sentence.

McGraw-Hill Language Arts
Grade 4, Unit 4, Adjectives,
pages 280–281

10

---

# Mechanics and Usage: Letter Punctuation

**RULES**

- The greeting and closing of a letter should begin with capital letters.
- Use a comma after the greeting and the closing of a friendly letter.
- Use a comma between the names of a city and a state.
- Use a comma between the day and the year in a date.

```
                                    237 Bridge Road
                                    Bangor, Maine ←city and state
                                    July 28, 2001 ←day and year
greeting→ Dear Maria,

        I just came back from vacation. My family
    and I went to Yellowstone National Park.
    I will tell you all about it when you visit.

                        Your friend, ←closing
                        Alana
```

Write each letter part. Add the correct punctuation mark or capital letter.

1. dear Uncle Joe,          **Dear Uncle Joe,**

2. Madison Wisconsin        **Madison, Wisconsin**

3. sincerely yours,         **Sincerely yours,**

4. dear friend              **Dear friend,**

5. May 7 2001               **May 7, 2001**

6. chicago illinois         **Chicago, Illinois**

7. your pal                 **Your pal,**

8. june 6 2001              **June 6, 2001**

9. dear mom                 **Dear Mom,**

10. your friend             **Your friend,**

At Home: Write a letter to a friend. Check to see if you punctuated and capitalized correctly.

McGraw-Hill Language Arts
Grade 4, Unit 4, Adjectives,
pages 282–283

10

## Mixed Review

### RULES

- An adjective can compare two people, places, or things:

  **adjective + -er**   *Soccer is a **faster** game than tennis.*

  **better** or **worse**   *I think soccer is **more exciting** than basketball.*

  **more + adjective**   *I play soccer **better** than baseball.*

- An adjective can compare more than two people, places, or things:

  **adjective + -est**   *We had the **fastest** team ever.*

  **most + adjective**   *Baseball is the **most popular** sport of all.*

  **best** or **worst**   *We had the **best** game of the season.*

- **Combine sentences** that tell about the same person, place, or thing.

  *Soccer is a game.    Soccer is fast.*
  *Soccer is a fast game.*

**A.** Write the correct form of the word or words in parentheses ( ).

1. Juan is (better, best) at soccer than I am.    **better**

2. Hector is the (stronger, strongest) player of all.    **strongest**

3. Megan is a (faster, fastest) runner than Tony.    **faster**

4. Yoshi had the (higher, highest) score on the team.    **highest**

5. This was my (worse, worst) year ever at baseball.    **worst**

**B.** Write each pair of sentences as one sentence.

6. The soccer game was about to begin. It was the last soccer game.
   The last soccer game was about to began.

7. We watched the soccer game. The soccer game was exciting.
   We watched the exciting soccer game.

8. We cheered for our team. Our team was winning.
   We cheered for our winning team.

9. Our team scored a point. It was the winning point.
   Our team scored the winning point.

10. The fans cheered the team. The team was victorious.
    The fans cheered the victorious team.

**At Home:** Write about a sport that you or some member of your family enjoys. Circle the adjectives that compare.

**McGraw-Hill Language Arts**
Grade 4, Unit 4, Mixed Review,
pages 284–285

---

## Common Errors: Adjectives

### RULES

- **short adjective + -er** compares two people, places, or things

  *Trees are **larger** than bushes.*

- **more + long adjective** compares two people, places, or things

  *Flowers are **more colorful** than leaves.*

- **adjective + -est** compare more than two people, places, or things

  *Trees are the **largest** plants.*

- **most + long adjective** compare more than two people, places, or things

  *I think orchids are the **most colorful** flowers.*

- Never use **more** or **most** with an adjective that already ends in **-er** or **-est**.

  *Wrong: Trees are **more larger** than bushes.*
  *Wrong: Trees are the **most largest** of all plants.*

Write the correct form of the adjective in parentheses ( ) on the line.

1. Bristlecone pine trees are the (old) living things on earth.    **oldest**

2. Giant sequoia trees are the (large) living things.    **largest**

3. Coconut seeds are the (big) of all seeds.    **biggest**

4. A cactus environment is (dry) than a woodland forest.    **drier**

5. A tropical rain forest is (wet) than a grassland.    **wetter**

6. Roses are the (beautiful) of all flowers.    **most beautiful**

7. Some orchids are the (rare) of all plants.    **rarest**

8. A tree is (tall) than a shrub.    **taller**

9. A baobob tree is (unusual) than an oak tree.    **more unusual**

10. A fern is (delicate) than a cactus.    **more delicate**

**At Home:** Look around your house or neighborhood for plants. Write sentences that compare them. Use the correct forms of the adjectives that compare.

**McGraw-Hill Language Arts**
Grade 4, Unit 4, Adjectives,
pages 286–287

## Study Skills: Maps

There are many kinds of maps.

- A **political map** shows how land is divided into states or countries.
- A **physical map** shows mountains, plains, deserts, bodies of water, and valleys.
- A **road map** shows roads in an area.

To understand a map, you can use the following:

- a **compass rose** to point out the directions north, south, east, and west.
- a **legend** or **key** to show the meanings of the symbols on the map.
- a **scale** to show how far it is from one place to another.

Study the map and then answer the questions below.

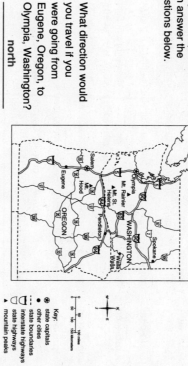

1. What direction would you travel if you were going from Eugene, Oregon, to Olympia, Washington?

   **north**

2. What are three mountain peaks on this map?

   **Mt. Hood, Mt. St. Helens, Mt. Rainier**

3. About how far in miles is it from Spokane, Washington, to Pendleton, Oregon?

   **about 150 miles**

4. About how far in kilometers is it from Pendleton, Oregon, to Walla Walla, Washington?

   **about 100 km**

5. What is the capital of Oregon? _____ **Salem**

**McGraw-Hill Language Arts**
Grade 4, Unit 4, Study Skills,
pages 294–295

**At Home:** Plan a trip from Eugene, Oregon, to Spokane, Washington. Write out a set of traveling directions and describe what you might see along the way.

65 [5]

---

## Vocabulary: Synonyms and Antonyms

- A **synonym** is a word that means the same or almost the same as another word.

  sad/gloomy    huge/enormous    pleasant/nice

- An **antonym** is a word that means the opposite of another word.

  happy/sad    big/small    right/wrong

After each pair of words, write **A** for antonyms or **S** for synonyms.

1. gigantic/enormous ___ **S**
2. fiction/nonfiction ___ **A**
3. messy/neat ___ **A**
4. baby/infant ___ **S**
5. old/aged ___ **S**
6. confused/muddled ___ **S**
7. narrow/wide ___ **A**
8. yell/shout ___ **S**
9. small/tiny ___ **S**
10. possess/own ___ **S**
11. moist/dry ___ **A**
12. angry/mad ___ **S**
13. fake/real ___ **A**
14. shiny/dull ___ **A**
15. stop/start ___ **A**
16. high/low ___ **A**
17. breezy/windy ___ **S**
18. opened/closed ___ **A**
19. slowly/quickly ___ **A**
20. quickly/speedily ___ **S**

**McGraw-Hill Language Arts**
Grade 4, Unit 4, Vocabulary,
pages 296–297

**At Home:** Write three pairs of synonyms and three pairs of antonyms. Use them in sentences.

66 [20]

## Composition: Organization

- Certain words and phrases can help you organize your ideas logically.
- Words like *inside, outside, over, beside, above, near, next to,* and *on top of* are **spatial words**. Spatial words tell where things are found or arranged.
- Words like *first, next, then, later, after that, as soon as,* and *a long time ago* are **time-order words**. They show when things happen and in what order.

Spatial order:   *Is the book beside the lamp or next to the CD player?*
Time order:      *As soon as your name is called, walk up to the stage.*

Underline spatial or time-order words used in each sentence. Then, circle **spatial** or **time-order** to identify the kind of words.

1. There's an eagle's nest on top of the cliff.   (**spatial**)   time-order

2. Which did you see first, the mole or the snake?   spatial   (**time-order**)

3. The mother alligator appeared, then a baby alligator followed.   spatial   (**time-order**)

4. Was it a long time ago that the cat had kittens?   spatial   (**time-order**)

5. An adult bird stands above the babies and feeds them worms.   (**spatial**)   time-order

6. Our canoe slid over the rocks and white water.   (**spatial**)   time-order

7. The horses happily graze near the barn.   (**spatial**)   time-order

8. Don't wait until later to feed the hungry chicks.   spatial   (**time-order**)

9. Is the corral behind the house or the barn?   (**spatial**)   time-order

10. After a long walk, we rested.   spatial   (**time-order**)

**At Home:** Write two sentences about your notebook. Organize one sentence with spatial words and the other with time-order words.

McGraw-Hill Language Arts
Grade 4, Unit 4, Composition Skills,
pages 296–297
10

---

## Pronouns

### RULES
- A **pronoun** is a word that replaces one or more nouns.
- A **pronoun** must agree with the noun it replaces.

That **boy** asked *if* **he** could dress up like a soldier.
singular noun   singular pronoun

The **soldiers** *did not realize* **they** *had no place to retreat.*
plural noun      plural pronoun

Underline the pronoun in each sentence. Then write each noun that the pronoun replaces.

1. Mrs. Harris said she will teach about the Civil War. _____ Mrs. Harris

2. The Battle of Antietam is remembered because it was an important battle of the Civil War. _____ Battle of Antietam

3. We talked about the generals and how they set out to win. _____ generals

4. General Robert E. Lee's soldiers didn't know they were in a bad position. _____ soldiers

5. The Union General George McClellan thought he would drive Lee's soldiers into the Potomac. _____ General George McClellan

6. General Stonewall Jackson's men must have been shocked when they were attacked by Union soldiers. _____ men

7. Jackson's lines were badly hurt and they were forced to retreat. _____ lines

8. The Confederates fled to the fields as they retreated from Union soldiers. _____ Confederates

9. Union soldiers were unaware of what they would soon be facing. _____ soldiers

10. Some historians consider the Battle of Antietam a Union victory although over two thousand soldiers died in it. _____ Battle of Antietam

**At Home:** Choose pronouns from this page. Use them in original sentences.

McGraw-Hill Language Arts
Grade 4, Unit 5, Pronouns,
pages 344–345
10

T34

## Subject Pronouns

**RULES**

- A **subject pronoun** is a pronoun that can be used as the subject of a sentence.

  **Singular:** *I, you, he, she, it*
  
  *I want to be a geologist.*
  
  **Plural:** *we, you, they*
  
  *They try to predict earthquakes and volcanic eruptions.*

Write a pronoun to replace the underlined subject part of each sentence.

1. <u>Dr. David Massaro</u> planned a unit about volcanoes for his science class. **He**

2. <u>Our class</u> just finished learning about earthquakes. **We**

3. <u>A volcano</u> is a destructive natural force. **It**

4. <u>The students in my class</u> learned that most volcanoes occur in an area called the Ring of Fire. **We**

5. <u>The volcanic eruptions</u> occur as a result of plate movements within the earth. **They**

6. <u>A volcano</u> releases hot poisonous gases into the air. **It**

7. <u>Some eruptions</u> form volcanic islands. **They**

8. <u>These mountain islands</u> build up from the ocean floor. **They**

9. <u>Valerie</u> wanted to know how far volcanic debris can travel. **She**

10. <u>The teacher</u> explained that erupting debris can travel for miles. **He**

11. <u>The lava from a volcano</u> can affect towns located miles away. **It**

12. <u>Mount St. Helens</u> violently erupted in 1980. **It**

13. <u>Many Washington citizens</u> were not prepared for this eruption. **They**

14. <u>The ashes</u> covered a huge area. **They**

15. <u>Scientists</u> are trying to predict when volcanoes will erupt. **They**

**At Home:** Rewrite the above sentences using the correct subject pronoun in place of the underlined words.

McGraw-Hill Language Arts
Grade 4, Unit 5, **Pronouns,**
pages 346–347

⬚ 15

---

## Object Pronouns

**RULES**

- **Object pronouns** generally appear in the predicate of a sentence.

  **Singular:** *me, you, him, her, it*
  
  **Plural:** *us, you, them*

- **Object pronouns** may be used after an action verb or after a word such as *for, at, of, with,* or *to.*

  *The teacher* <u>made</u> **our class** *write a report. The teacher* <u>made</u> **us** *write a report.*
  
  *Students cooperated* <u>with</u> **the teacher**. *Students cooperated* <u>with</u> **her**.

Underline the object pronoun in each sentence and write it on the line.

1. You warned me this class would be hard. **me**

2. I told you to plan wisely. **you**

3. Mrs. McMadden gave them work to do. **them**

4. They didn't expect her to assign a project so soon. **her**

5. She had a report for me to write. **me**

6. The teacher chose the topics for us. **us**

7. Students wondered what topic she would give them. **them**

8. Jimmy said he would ask her for an easy subject. **her**

9. Mrs. McMadden said she was not happy with him. **him**

10. He looked at her with a confused expression. **her**

11. She wanted him to change his attitude. **him**

12. After the teacher gave the topics to them, they were relieved. **them**

13. Each of us had the same topic. **us**

14. They thought that was very kind of her. **her**

15. Now I can work with you on the project. **you**

**At Home:** Make up sentences using the object pronouns *me, us, you, him, her,* or *them.* Say your sentences aloud to a family member.

McGraw-Hill Language Arts
Grade 4, Unit 5, **Pronouns,**
pages 348–349

⬚ 15

# Mechanics and Usage: Punctuation in Dialogue

## RULES

**Dialogue** is the exact words spoken by the characters in a story.

- Always use quotation marks at the beginning and end of dialogue.
- Begin a speaker's words with a capital letter.

  Mother said, *"Let's plan a vacation!"*

  *"We can go camping,"* Dad suggested.

- Begin a new paragraph whenever a new person speaks.

  *"The National Parks are always fun. Maybe we'll even see a bear at our campsite!"* Jamie exclaimed.

  *"I'd rather stay in a hotel,"* Sean whined.

Write the letter C before the dialogue that is written correctly.

1. __C__ Dad said, "Camping would save us some money."

   ____ "Dad said, camping would save us some money."

2. __C__ "Gee, Dad. We've been saving for this trip all year," Mom said.

   ____ Gee, Dad. "We've been saving for this trip all year." Mom said.

3. ____ Well, how about a compromise? "He suggested."

   __C__ "Well, how about a compromise?" he suggested.

4. __C__ "We could stay in a hotel on our way to one of the National Parks. Does that sound like a good idea?" Dad asked.

   ____ "We could stay in a hotel on our way to one of the National Parks. "Does that sound like a good idea?" Dad asked.

5. ____ Mom replied, Let's hear what our children have to say about it."

   __C__ Mom replied, "Let's hear what the children have to say about it."

   ____ "I'll go along with it, as long as I get to camp out!" said Sean.

   __C__ "I'll go along with it, as long as I get to camp out!" said Sean.

McGraw-Hill Language Arts
Grade 4, Unit 5, Pronouns,
pages 350–351

**At Home:** Ask your family to plan a trip. Write down a few sentences of your family's dialogue.

 5

---

# Mixed Review

## RULES

- A **subject pronoun** is used as the subject of a sentence.

  **Singular:** *I, you, he, she, it* → *She* wants to go to New York City.

  **Plural:** *we, you, they* → *We* were planning our summer vacation.

- An **object pronoun** is used after an action verb or a word such as *in, into, to, with, for, by,* or *at.*

  **Singular:** *me, you, him, her, it* → They asked *me* where I wanted to go.

  **Plural:** *us, you, them* → Who is going to go with *us?*

- Use **quotation marks** before and after a person's exact words.

  *"I would like to go someplace unusual,"* I said.

Rewrite each sentence. Replace each underlined noun with the correct pronoun. Add quotation marks and capital letters where needed.

1. Mom said, let's go to the Statue of Liberty.

   She said, "Let's go to the Statue of Liberty."

2. the Statue of Liberty is in New York City, she told us.

   "It is in New York City," she told us.

3. it was given to the united states by france, Dad explained.

   "It was given to the United States by France," he explained.

4. your mother and i saw it many years ago, he said.

   "We saw it many years ago," he said.

5. this summer might be a good time for the family to go, Dad suggested.

   "This summer might be a good time for us to go," Dad suggested.

McGraw-Hill Language Arts
Grade 4, Unit 5, Mixed Review,
pages 352–353

**At Home:** Think of some place you have visited with your family. Make up a conversation about it with one of your family members. Use some subject and object pronouns in your conversation. Punctuate correctly.

 5

## Pronoun-Verb Agreement

**RULES**

- Add **-s** or **-es** to most action verbs in the present tense when using the pronouns *he, she,* or *it.*

  *He* **wins** the prize.          *She* **watches** happily.

- When using the pronouns *I, we, you,* or *they,* do not add **-s** or **-es** to a present tense action verb.

  *You* **ride** the bike.          *I* **watch** the race.

Circle the correct verb in parentheses that agrees with the subject pronoun.

TRIATHALON 〜 Swim 〜 Bike 〜 Run

1. He (plan, plans) to run in the triathlon this weekend.

2. She (train, trains) for the race also.

3. We (hope, hopes) one of them will be able to win.

4. At first, they (swim, swims) in the lake for 1.5 miles.

5. Then they (ride, rides) their bikes from the park to the center of town.

6. Finally, it (end, ends) with a three-mile run through the streets downtown.

7. We (hope, hopes) to watch the entire race.

8. They (start, starts) the competition at 7:00 A.M. sharp.

9. It (take, takes) over an hour to complete the course.

10. She (race, races) toward the finish line.

**At Home:** Write a paragraph about a time you were in some kind of competition. Use subject pronouns in your account.

McGraw-Hill Language Arts
Grade 4, Unit 5, Pronouns,
pages 354–355

☐ / 10

---

## Combining Sentences

**RULES**

- You can **combine sentences** that have similar ideas by joining **pronouns** in either the subject or the predicate.

  She planned a class party. I planned a class party.
  **She and I** planned a class party.

Combine each pair of sentences. Use *and* or *or.*

1. She will make the decorations. I will make the decorations.
   She and I will make the decorations.

2. Does the scissors belong to you? Does the scissors belong to them?
   Does the scissors belong to you or them?

3. You want to help plan the menu. I want to help plan the menu.
   You and I want to help plan the menu.

4. You should call the class officers. I should call the class officers.
   You and I should call the class officers.

5. Did he return our phone calls? Did she return our phone calls?
   Did he or she return our phone calls?

6. You can invite former teachers. I can invite former teachers.
   You and I can invite former teachers.

7. I might not recognize him. I might not recognize her.
   I might not recognize him or her.

8. Tim will give a balloon to you. Tim will give a balloon to me.
   Tim will give a balloon to you and me.

9. He will be glad to see you. He will be glad to see me.
   He will be glad to see you and me.

10. Will he be able to attend? Will she be able to attend?
    Will he or she be able to attend?

**At Home:** Find three sentences above that can be combined using the word *we.*

McGraw-Hill Language Arts
Grade 4, Unit 5, Pronouns,
pages 356–357

☐ / 10

## Possessive Pronouns

**RULES**

- A **possessive pronoun** is a pronoun that shows ownership by one or more persons, places, or things.

| my | your | his | her | its | our |
| their | mine | ours | hers | yours | theirs |

- Some possessive pronouns can be used alone.
  *These are* **Keri's** *fossils.* *These are* **hers.**

Choose a possessive pronoun from the box above that means the same as the words in parentheses.

1. Is this _____ book about fossils? (belonging to you)  **your**

2. Who is _____ author? (belonging to it)  **its**

3. Gina Larocca is _____ name. (belonging to a female)  **her**

4. Collecting fossils is a favorite hobby of _____ . (belonging to me)  **mine**

5. One of _____ teachers in the fourth grade has a display of mold and cast fossils. (belonging to us)  **our**

6. She will show us how to make mold fossils like _____ . (belonging to her)  **hers**

7. Her mold fossils were made when animals left _____ footprints in a patch of muddy soil. (belonging to them)  **their**

8. _____ will be made by making imprints of leaves on soft clay. (belonging to us)  **ours**

9. The other science classes will be making hand imprints in plaster to create _____ . (belonging to them)  **theirs**

10. George will try to make a cast fossil from the imprint of _____ hand by using it as a mold. (belonging to him)  **his**

**At Home:** Choose five possessive pronouns from the box above. Make up a sentence for each. Say the sentences aloud to a parent or sister or brother.

McGraw-Hill Language Arts
Grade 4, Unit 5, Pronouns,
pages 358–359

10

---

## Mechanics and Usage: Contractions—Pronouns and Verbs

**RULES**

- A pronoun and a verb can be combined to form a **contraction**.
  *She is*   **She's**   *You are*   **You're**   *We have*   **We've**
- The contractions **it's, you're,** and **they're** should not be confused with the possessive pronouns **its, your,** and **their.**
  *It's time to give your dog* ***its*** *bath.*
  *You're going to need to bring* ***your*** *supply of towels.*
  *You will find that* ***they're*** *in* ***their*** *proper place on the shelf.*

Underline the word in parentheses that correctly completes the sentence.

1. (Your, You're) lucky that you were not born in the early 1800s.

2. (It's, Its) the time when Americans were trying to extend the frontier.

3. (You've, You're) probably heard about the hard life of the pioneers.

4. (They're, They'd) travel westward by wagon trains.

5. (Its, It's) hard to imagine traveling by wagon train across the Great Plains.

6. The American frontier has many heroes in (its, it's) history.

7. (We're, We've) all heard of Daniel Boone and Davy Crockett.

8. (They're, Their) two of the most famous frontiersmen.

9. Boone explored Kentucky for the pioneers and blazed (they're, their) trails.

10. (His, He's) known as a generous leader who led westward-moving settlers through a route called The Wilderness Road.

11. (It's, Its) a route through rugged parts of the Appalachian Mountains.

12. (You're, Your) teacher may have told you about Davy Crockett.

13. (We've, We're) come to associate Davy Crockett's name with the Alamo.

14. These famous frontiersmen tamed the wilderness through (their, they're) hard work.

15. (Your, You're) library's encyclopedia has more information about them.

**At Home:** Write sentences correctly using the words *its, it's, they're, their, you're,* and *your.*

McGraw-Hill Language Arts
Grade 4, Unit 5, Pronouns,
pages 360–361

15

## Mixed Review

**RULES**

- **Present tense verbs** must agree with their **subject pronouns.**

  **Singular Subject Pronouns:** *I, you, he, she, it*    *He travels on weekends.*
  **Plural Subject Pronouns:**    *we, you, they*    *They travel on weekends.*

- A **possessive pronoun** takes the place of one or more possessive nouns.

  *Cindy's piano teacher was very good. Her piano teacher was very good.*

  **Singular Possessive Pronouns:** *my, yours, his, her, its*
  **Plural Possessive Pronouns:**    *our, your, their*

- A **contraction** is a shortened form of two words, such as a pronoun and a verb. An apostrophe (') shows the missing letters.

  *I'm = I am*    *we're = we are*    *they'll = they will*

- Don't confuse the contractions *it's, they're,* and *you're* with the possessive pronouns *its, their,* and *your.*

Rewrite each sentence. Form contractions from the underlined pronouns and verbs. Substitute possessive pronouns for underlined possessive nouns.

1. It is going to be fun at Mike's party this weekend.
   <u>It's going to be fun at Mike's party this weekend.</u>

2. We are going to see my brother's Little League game.
   <u>We're going to see his Little League game.</u>

3. They have bought tickets for my sister's talent show.
   <u>They've bought tickets for her talent show.</u>

4. She is going to see Betty's new house.
   <u>She's going to see her new house.</u>

5. We have some time before John's piano recital begins.
   <u>We've some time before his piano recital begins.</u>

**At Home:** Write five sentences about things your family likes to do on weekends. Include some possessive pronouns and contractions. Be sure the verbs and subjects in your sentences agree.

McGraw-Hill Language Arts
Grade 4, Unit 5, Mixed Review,
pages 362–363

5

---

## Common Errors: Pronouns

**RULES**

- Use a **subject pronoun** as the subject of a sentence.

  **Singular:** *I, you, he, she, it*
  **Plural:** *we, you, they*

- Use an **object pronoun** after an action verb or after words such as *for, at, of, with, in, to,* or *by.*

  **Singular:** *me, you, him, her, it*
  **Plural:** *us, you, them*

  *I always wanted to learn how to swim.    I found a course just right for **me.***

- **Possessive pronouns** do not have apostrophes.

  *The course is famous for **its** success.*

Write a pronoun to take the place of the underlined words.

1. <u>Mario and I</u> took swimming lessons last summer.    **We**

2. <u>The lessons</u> lasted for six weeks.    **They**

3. A local hotel loaned us <u>the hotel's</u> pool.    **its**

4. <u>The pool</u> was almost olympic size.    **It**

5. <u>The instructor</u> was a teacher from our school.    **He**

6. He helped <u>Mario</u> to relax in the water.    **him**

7. <u>Mario and me</u> were swimming in no time.    **We**

8. We were able to keep up with the rest <u>of the class.</u>    **them**

9. Everyone was surprised at <u>Mario</u> for taking the course.    **him**

10. <u>His family and friends</u> talked him into it.    **They**

**At Home:** Write about something you learned to do. Include at least three sentences that have pronouns.

McGraw-Hill Language Arts
Grade 4, Unit 5, Pronouns,
pages 364–365

10

## Study Skills: Dictionary

- **A dictionary** shows the spelling, meaning, and pronunciation of words.
  - **Guide words** indicate the first and last words on a page. They appear at the top of each dictionary page.
  - **A pronunciation key** shows how to say words. It usually appears at the bottom of every other page.
  - **Entry words** are the words explained in the dictionary. They appear in alphabetical order.
- Every entry word includes:
  - the **pronunciation** of the word
  - the **part of speech** (shown as an abbreviation, like *n., v., adj., adv.*—noun, verb, adjective, adverb)
  - one or more **definitions** (sometimes with **example sentences**).

Use the part of the dictionary page below to answer the questions. Underline the correct answer.

> **foil** (foil) *n.* **1.** a very thin sheet of metal. **2.** something that makes another thing seem better when compared [Martha acted as a *foil* when she shouted out the correct answer before Henry could be called on.] **3.** a thin sword with a guard over the point to prevent injury when used in fencing.

1. Which pair of words could be the guide words on this dictionary page?

   fly /folk          fluffy/focus

2. What does the letter *n* stand for in the dictionary entry?

   no pronunciation available          the word is a noun

3. How many definitions are there for the word *foil*?

   2          3

4. Where would you look to find the pronunciation key?

   on bottom of this or the next page          next to the guide words

5. Which definition of *foil* has an example sentence?

   1          2          3

McGraw-Hill Language Arts
Grade 4, Unit 5, Study Skills,
pages 372–373

5

---

McGraw-Hill School Division

## Vocabulary: Homophones and Homographs

- **Homophones** are pairs of words that sound alike but are spelled differently and mean different things.

  fare/fair    cents/sense    minor/miner    scene/seen

- **Homographs** are words that are spelled alike but have different meanings. They may be pronounced differently, too.

  *I opened the **trunk** of the car.    The elephant's **trunk** would not fit.*
  *The tree **trunk** was in our way.*

Underline the two words in each sentence that are either homophones or homographs. Then write *homophones* or *homographs* to tell what kind of words they are.

1. It isn't fair that I can't show my pet pig at the fair. _____ homographs

2. My eyes were tearing as I began tearing up my entry fee. _____ homographs

3. "Bye," I said to the judge as she passed by. _____ homophones

4. "Would you help me cut this pile of wood?" _____ homophones

5. "My saw was here a minute ago, I know I saw it." _____ homographs

6. "Next week I will cut the weak tree limb." _____ homophones

7. "I can go get you a sandwich and a can of soda." _____ homographs

8. "Stay here, Gramps," I said, "I can hear the food vendor coming this way." _____ homophones

9. When we were just about through, Dad threw an old flour sack at my feet. _____ homophones

10. They're all waiting for their champion sack racer," he said. "Let's all go." _____ homophones

McGraw-Hill Language Arts
Grade 4, Unit 5, Vocabulary,
pages 374–375

10

## Composition: Writing Dialogue

- Dialogue is the part of a story that shows the conversation among characters.
- The exact words a character says have **quotation marks** around them.
- The first word inside of an opening quotation mark is **capitalized.**
- End punctuation appears before a closing quotation mark.
- Words like *said Winston* or *she explained* help the reader know which character is speaking the words in a dialogue.
- Every time a different character speaks, begin a new paragraph.

Tommy explained, "This is a model of an early airplane." Then he asked Sara, "Do you like it?"

Sara exclaimed, "It's wonderful. May I help you build your next model, Tommy?"

"Of course you can. We'll have a great time," Tommy said.

Read the story. Underline every group of words spoken by story characters.

**1.–10.** Raymond pushed the door open slowly and said, "Mom, how will I know which puppy to choose?"

Mrs. Botera thought for a minute and answered, "It's not an easy decision. I think, though, that you'll just know which puppy is right as soon as you meet it." She followed Raymond through the door into a hall lined with kennel cages. "Look, Raymond, a puppy with black spots!" Mrs. Botera directed her son's attention.

Raymond saw the dog and said, "It looks like our old dog Jed." Raymond asked the attendant to let him see the white puppy with the black spots. "The spots are smaller, but this dog seems just as friendly as good old Jed," Raymond added.

"The dog is a Dalmatian," the attendant told Raymond as the puppy tumbled into Raymond's arms. "It needs to run a lot, but it can be a wonderful pet."

Raymond said, "I'll run with it every day because I'm on my school's track team." He and his mother petted the little dog. Raymond thought for awhile. "Let's call him Jed II!" he exclaimed.

**At Home:** Write dialogue that shows a conversation you might have with someone about choosing a new pet. Remember to follow the rules for dialogue from the box on this page.

McGraw-Hill Language Arts
Grade 4, Unit 5, Composition Skills,
pages 376–377

10

---

## Adverbs That Tell *How*

**RULES**

- An **adverb** is a word that tells more about a verb. Adverbs can tell how something happened. Many adverbs end in *-ly.*

Earthquakes *happen* **suddenly.**

**verb**        **adverb** (tells how)

Write the adverb that describes each underlined verb.

1. An earthquake really <u>scares</u> most people. _____ really

2. Scientists can rarely <u>tell</u> when one will strike. _____ rarely

3. Earthquakes generally <u>occur</u> along faults. _____ generally

4. Mom <u>described</u> it simply as a large crack in the bedrock. _____ simply

5. Rocks normally <u>move</u> in opposite directions along a fault. _____ normally

6. Pressure easily <u>builds</u> as rocks push against one another. _____ easily

7. Pressure suddenly <u>releases</u> when one rock slips past the other. _____ suddenly

8. The sudden release of energy usually <u>causes</u> vibrations. _____ usually

9. The vibrations <u>travel</u> quickly in waves. _____ quickly

10. In California, vibrations or tremors <u>occur</u> regularly. _____ regularly

11. The ground <u>vibrates</u> slowly. _____ slowly

12. Unsecured things quickly <u>fall</u> to the ground. _____ quickly

13. Some broken gas lines <u>explode</u> violently. _____ violently

14. People clearly <u>understand</u> the dangers an earthquake may bring. _____ clearly

15. They wisely <u>prepare</u> ahead of time by learning good safety rules. _____ wisely

**At Home:** Choose any five adverbs that you wrote above and use them in sentences. Say your sentences aloud to a member of your family.

McGraw-Hill Language Arts
Grade 4, Unit 6, Adverbs,
pages 420–421

15

## Adverbs That Tell *When* or *Where*

**RULES**

- You already know that an **adverb** tells more about a verb, such as **how** something happened. An adverb can also tell **where** or **when** an action takes place.

*Kara, drive **slowly**!* (how)
*Look **outside**.* (where)
*The trees are changing colors **now**.* (when)

Underline the adverb in each sentence. Write whether the adverb tells *when*, *where*, or *how* about the action that is taking place.

1. The end of summer comes quickly. _____ how

2. Breezes carry the fallen leaves far. _____ where

3. Many people enjoy activities outdoors. _____ where

4. Apples, gourds, and pumpkins are in orchards nearby. _____ where

5. Travelers also plan car trips then. _____ when

6. Motorists drive slowly in the countryside. _____ how

7. Colorful trees appear everywhere. _____ where

8. Maple leaves often turn bright orange or red. _____ when

9. Sometimes they turn bright yellow. _____ when

10. People always enjoy the brilliant colors. _____ when

11. The colorful leaves do not stay forever. _____ when

12. Soon the trees are bare. _____ when

13. Colder weather will come soon. _____ when

14. Heavy snows will fall later. _____ when

15. People usually stay indoors during a big snowstorm. _____ where

**At Home:** Rewrite three of the above sentences using different adverbs. For example: *Heavy snows will fall soon.*

McGraw-Hill Language Arts
Grade 4, Unit 6, Adverbs,
pages 422–423

15

---

## Adverbs That Compare

**RULES**

- **Adverbs** can be used to make comparisons.
- Add *-er* to short adverbs to compare two actions. Add *-est* to compare more than two actions.

*Stephanie swims **fast** at practice.*
*Stephanie swims **faster** than Paula.*
*Stephanie swims **fastest** of all the swimmers on the team.*

Write the adverb in parentheses that correctly completes the sentence.

1. I joined the swim team _____ later _____ this year than I did last year. (later, latest)

2. Swim team fees dropped _____ lower _____ than they were last year. (lowest, lower)

3. Our team, the Sharks, practices _____ earlier _____ in the morning than the Waves team. (earliest, earlier)

4. The Sharks practice _____ longer _____ than the Waves. (longer, longest)

5. Of all the practices and meets, most teams swim _____ hardest at a championship meet. (harder, hardest)

6. Jessica does the butterfly stroke _____ slower _____ than Yolanda. (slower, slowest)

7. Our best swimmers kick _____ hardest _____. (harder, hardest)

8. Backstroke swimmers who have long strokes swim _____ faster than those with short strokes. (fastest, faster)

9. Olympic stars swim _____ fastest _____ of all. (fastest, faster)

10. Many champions begin training _____ sooner _____ than average swimmers. (sooner, soonest)

**At Home:** Tell a family member how you knew which adverb to choose for your answer in the above sentences.

McGraw-Hill Language Arts
Grade 4, Unit 6, Adverbs,
pages 424–425

10

## More Adverbs That Compare

### RULES

- The words *more* and *most* are usually used to form comparisons with adverbs that end in -ly and with longer adverbs.
- Use *more* to compare two actions.

  *A river raft changes its course **more abruptly** in rapids than in a gentle stream.*

- Use *most* to compare more than two actions.

  *Of all white water, class VI rapids churn **most powerfully**.*

Underline the word in parentheses that completes each sentence correctly.

1. Water flows (more, <u>most</u>) slowly on level ground than in the mountains.

2. Mountain streams flow (more, <u>most</u>) quickly of all.

3. The Gauley River in West Virginia runs (more, most) swiftly than the Ocoee River in Tennessee.

4. River guides paddle (more, most) cautiously through rapids than through other moving water.

5. Of all times, rafters smile (more, <u>most</u>) happily at the end of a safe trip.

6. Compared with all other sports enthusiasts, kayakers play (more, most) dangerously.

7. Kayakers paddle (<u>more</u>, most) vigorously than rafters.

8. A well-trained guide travels the river (more, <u>most</u>) easily of all river runners.

9. Some river outfitters operate (more, most) safely than others.

10. Of all sports groups, they train their employees (more, <u>most</u>) rigorously.

**At Home:** Write two original sentences using adverbs with the words *more* and *most*.

McGraw-Hill Language Arts
Grade 4, Unit 6, Adverbs,
pages 426–427

10

---

## Mechanics and Usage: *Good and Well*

### RULES

- Use the adjective *good* when describing a noun.

  *It is wise to make **good** decisions.*

- Use the adverb *well* when telling more about a verb.

  *You will do **well** if you make wise decisions.*

Write the letter **C** before the sentence that uses *good* or *well* correctly.

1. C _____ Ryan's parents are glad that he makes good choices.
   _____ Ryan's parents are glad that he makes well choices.

2. C _____ His teachers say he listens good at school.
   _____ His teachers say he listens well at school.

3. C _____ They noticed that he chooses friends good.
   _____ They noticed that he chooses friends well.

4. C _____ His parents agree that he has good friends.
   _____ His parents agree that he has well friends.

5. C _____ They also think that his grades are good.
   _____ They also think that his grades are well.

6. C _____ He remembers good in history class, but not in math.
   _____ He remembers well in history class, but not in math.

7. C _____ His idea about doing homework in study hall was a good one.
   _____ His idea about doing homework in study hall was a well one.

8. C _____ He eats at least three good meals a day and gets plenty of rest.
   _____ He eats at least three well meals a day and gets plenty of rest.

9. C _____ Ryan should expect a well report card.
   _____ Ryan should expect a good report card.

10. C _____ His teachers and parents are happy that he is progressing so good.
    _____ His teachers and parents are happy that he is progressing so well.

**At Home:** Write a sentence that tells what you do well. Then write a sentence that tells what is good about it. For example: *I ride a bike well. Riding a bike gives me good exercise.*

McGraw-Hill Language Arts
Grade 4, Unit 6, Adverbs,
pages 428–429

10

# Mixed Review

## RULES

- An **adverb** tells more about a verb. Adverbs tell *how, when,* or *where* an action takes place.

  We **gladly** went to the county fair.     **tells how**

  I **never** miss going with my friends.     **tells when**

  It is held **here** every year in the fall.     **tells where**

- Add *-er* to short adverbs to compare two actions. Add *-est* to compare more than two actions.

  My horse jumped **higher** than her horse.

  Of all the horses, this one jumped the **highest**.

- The words *more* and *most* are usually used to form comparisons with longer adverbs and adverbs that end in *-y.*

  This horse ran **more quickly** than that horse.

  Of all the horses, this one ran the **most quickly**.

Circle the adverb that correctly completes each sentence. Write whether the adverb tells *how, when,* or *where.*

1. Our county fair (usually) attracts many people.     _____ when

2. I arrived (earlier) at the fair than my friend Emma.     _____ when

3. We (gleefully) watch many of the events.     _____ how

4. Mike eats the (most) in the hot dog eating contest.     _____ how

5. The pig race draws a large crowd (here).     _____ where

6. Mr. Jenson's pig runs the (most quickly) of all.     _____ how

7. Mark (confidently) enters the frog jumping contest.     _____ how

8. The frog that jumps the (farthest) of all wins a prize.     _____ where

9. My frog (never) wins the jumping contest.     _____ when

10. We left the fair more (reluctantly) than we did last year.     _____ how

**At Home:** Talk to family members or friends about the most unusual contest they have seen. Write a paragraph about it. Circle each adverb you include.

McGraw-Hill Language Arts
Grade 4, Unit 6, Mixed Review,
pages 430–431

10

---

# Negatives

## RULES

- **Negatives** are words that mean "no." Usually they contain the word *no* or a contraction for *not,* such as: *not, nobody, nowhere, none, no one.*

- Never use more than one negative at a time in a sentence.

  **INCORRECT:** *I can't make no decisions.*

  **CORRECT:** *I can't make any decisions.*

Underline the double negatives in each sentence. Then rewrite the sentence correctly by replacing one of the negatives with the word in parentheses.

1. There isn't nothing worse than being the new kid at school. (is)
   There is nothing worse than being the new kid at school.

2. It feels like I'm not never going to make any friends. (ever)
   It feels like I'm not ever going to make any friends.

3. I thought I told you I didn't know nobody at school. (anybody)
   I thought I told you I didn't know anybody at school.

4. I guess that nobody listens to me no more. (anymore)
   I guess that nobody listens to me anymore.

5. By now you should understand why I can't invite no one over. (anyone)
   By now you should understand why I can't invite anyone over.

6. You know I don't like going nowhere alone. (anywhere)
   You know I don't like going anywhere alone.

7. There aren't no teachers around to help make the introductions. (are)
   There are no teachers around to help make the introductions.

8. Isn't there nothing I can do about this? (something)
   Isn't there something I can do about this?

9. I am not trying nothing new until I make at least one new friend. (anything)
   I am not trying anything new until I make at least one new friend.

10. We aren't moving nowhere ever again! (anywhere)
    We aren't moving anywhere ever again!

**At Home:** Rewrite sentences 1, 5, and 7 a different way without changing the meaning. Replace the other negative instead.

McGraw-Hill Language Arts
Grade 4, Unit 6, Adverbs,
pages 432–433

10

McGraw-Hill School Division

## Prepositions

**RULES**

• A **preposition** is a word that comes before a noun or a pronoun and relates it to another word in a sentence. Here are some prepositions:

| about | over | from | in | for |
|-------|------|------|-----|-----|
| above | under | through | across | |
| after | behind | until | on | |
| by | near | with | off | |

Underline the preposition in each sentence.

1. Lisa decided she would wear a red sweater <u>over</u> her blouse.

2. First, she looked <u>in</u> the dresser where she keeps her sweaters.

3. She found her red sweater <u>with</u> the others.

4. It was <u>under</u> her favorite blue sweater.

5. Then she spotted her gray sweater <u>across</u> the room.

6. The beautiful gray sweater was sitting <u>on</u> the floor.

7. This sweater was a gift <u>from</u> her Aunt Marge.

8. Aunt Marge would be disappointed if she knew <u>about</u> this.

9. Lisa quickly lifted the sweater <u>off</u> the floor.

10. For a brief moment, Lisa thought she would wear the gray sweater.

11. Lisa donned the sweater and then looked <u>in</u> the mirror.

12. She decided the gray sweater didn't look good <u>with</u> this outfit.

13. She tied the red sweater <u>around</u> her waist.

14. Lisa turned and looked <u>at</u> her reflection again.

15. This is exactly what Lisa would wear <u>to</u> the school dance.

McGraw-Hill Language Arts
Grade 4, Unit 6, Adverbs,
pages 434–435

/15

**At Home:** Write several versions of sentence three. Each time, use a different preposition and noun or pronoun to tell where she found the red sweater. For example, *She found her red sweater* ***on the bed.***

---

## Prepositional Phrases

**RULES**

• A **prepositional phrase** is a group of words that begins with a preposition and ends with a noun or pronoun.

*There are many hot springs and geysers **inside** the park.*

Write the prepositional phrase and underline the noun or pronoun that it ends with.

1. Our family went to Yellowstone National Park.
   to Yellowstone National Park

2. Our best friends traveled with us. _____ with <u>us</u>

3. First, we flew a plane into Salt Lake City. _____ into Salt Lake <u>City</u>

4. Then we borrowed a rental van from an agency. _____ from an <u>agency</u>

5. We spent about a day exploring the Great Salt Lake. _____ about a <u>day</u>

6. The huge lake was filled with shrimp. _____ with <u>shrimp</u>

7. We left and headed for Wyoming. _____ for <u>Wyoming</u>

8. Driving across Utah was interesting. _____ across <u>Utah</u>

9. Next we passed through Idaho. _____ through <u>Idaho</u>

10. We finally arrived in a town called Jackson. _____ in a <u>town</u>

11. Jackson, Wyoming, is the home of Grand Teton National Park.
    of Grand Teton National Park

12. Yellowstone National Park is north of this area. _____ of this <u>area</u>

13. We headed toward the Tetons. _____ toward the <u>Tetons</u>

14. We arrived at Yellowstone. _____ at <u>Yellowstone</u>

15. Once inside the park, we visited Old Faithful and other interesting volcanic features. _____ inside the <u>park</u>

McGraw-Hill Language Arts
Grade 4, Unit 6, Adverbs,
pages 436–437

/15

**At Home:** List the prepositions you wrote in the above exercises.

## Combining Sentences: Complex Sentences

**RULES**

- A **complex sentence** contains two related sentences that have been combined with a conjunction other than *and*, *but*, or *or*.
- You can combine two short sentences to form a complex sentence.
  *Some people harvest saguaro fruit. It makes good preserves.*
  *Some people harvest saguaro fruit because it makes good preserves.*

Combine the short sentences into one complex sentence by using a conjunction from the box. Don't forget correct punctutation. Answers may vary.

| because | before | although | if | unless | until |
|---------|--------|----------|-----|--------|-------|
| | | wherever | when | while | |

1. You will see the desert. You travel to Arizona.
   You will see the desert if you travel to Arizona.

2. Be sure to go on a hike. You are there.
   Be sure to go on a hike while you are there.

3. You will see cactus. You hike in the desert.
   You will see cactus wherever you hike in the desert.

4. Bring bottled water. There is no water available.
   Bring bottled water, because there is no water available.

5. I never saw a saguaro cactus. I visited Tucson.
   I never saw a saguaro cactus before I visited Tucson.

6. You may not see this cactus. You go there.
   Unless you go there, you may not see this cactus.

7. The saguaro looks like a barrel. It is very young.
   The saguaro looks like a barrel when it is very young.

8. Arms don't grow. The cactus is more mature.
   Arms don't grow until the cactus is more mature.

9. They have flowers and fruit. Saguaros don't have leaves.
   Saguaros don't have flowers and fruit, although they have flowers and fruit.

10. Desert creatures eat its ripe pulp. The fruit splits open.
    Desert creatures eat its ripe pulp when the fruit splits open.

**At Home:** Find a complex sentence in a local newspaper. Break it down into two separate sentences.

McGraw-Hill Language Arts
Grade 4, Unit 6, Adverbs,
pages 438–439   `10`

---

## Mechanics and Usage: Commas

**RULES**

- A **comma** shows a pause in your writing.
  *No, I didn't realize the five senses are part of our nervous system.*
- Use a comma to set off the name of the person you are speaking to.
  *David, didn't you listen in health class?*
- Use a comma to set off an introductory word.
  *Well, it's time you started to pay attention.*

Insert commas where needed.

1. Betsy, don't touch that hot stove!

2. Phillip, why are you shouting at me?

3. Well, you were about to burn your fingers!

4. Yes, but I would have pulled my hand quickly away.

5. Sure, but not quickly enough to keep from getting hurt.

6. Thank you for caring enough to warn me, Phillip.

7. Did you know, Betsy, that your fingertips can send a message to your brain?

8. Yes, but how does the message get there?

9. The messages travel through special nerve cells called neurons, Betsy.

10. That sounds interesting, Phillip.

11. For example, neurons in your fingers sense that the stove is hot.

12. Next, the message is translated as an electronic impulse.

13. Phillip, that sounds amazing!

14. Finally, the impulse travels across a network of nerve cells all the way to your brain.

15. Yes, I've heard that's how it works.

`15`   McGraw-Hill Language Arts
Grade 4, Unit 6, Adverbs,
pages 440–441

**At Home:** Ask a family member to use your name as they speak directly to you. Write the first few sentences of your conversation.

# Mixed Review

## RULES

- A **negative** means "no." Never use two negatives in one sentence.

  I have not never been on an airplane.

- A **preposition**, such as *about*, *of*, *with*, *to*, *through*, *upon*, comes before a noun or pronoun and links it to the rest of the sentence.

  The airport was full *of* people.

- A **prepositional phrase** is a group of words that begins with a preposition and ends in a noun or pronoun.

  I walked eagerly *toward the plane.*

- A **complex sentence** combines two ideas by using words that tell where, when, why, how, and under what circumstances.

  I was very excited. I walked onto the plane.

  I was very excited *when* I walked onto the plane.

**A.** Combine each pair of sentences into a complex sentence. Correct any double negatives.

1. I was worried about flying. I was in the air.
   I was worried about flying until I was in the air.

2. I couldn't never tell we were moving. We flew through the sky.
   I couldn't tell we were moving as we flew through the sky.

3. We landed smoothly. We reached our destination.
   We landed smoothly when we reached our destination.

4. I don't never like to fly. The weather is bad.
   I never like to fly when the weather is bad.

5. I enjoy flying. It is very exciting for me.
   I enjoy flying because it is very exciting for me.

**B. 6.–10.** Underline five prepositional phrases in the complex sentences you wrote.

**At Home:** Think about when you did something for the first time. Write a paragraph describing what it was like. Circle each prepositional phrase you use. Check to see if you can combine any sentences.

McGraw-Hill Language Arts
Grade 4, Unit 6, Mixed Review, pages 442–443

🔟

---

# Common Errors: Adverbs

## RULES

- An **adjective** describes a noun. An **adverb** tells more about a verb.

  I put the *little* puzzle together *quickly.*

- *Good* is an adjective. *Well* is an adverb.

  My *good* friend and I work *well* together.

- Do not use two negative words together in a sentence.

  They could *not* find *any* puzzles to do.

- Many adverbs are formed by adding *-ly* to an adjective. For most adverbs, do not change the spelling of the base word when you add *-ly.*

  We *finally* found a puzzle we liked.

Write the word in parentheses ( ) that completes each sentence correctly.

1. I (recent, recently) finished putting another jigsaw puzzle together. _____ recently

2. I (frequent, frequently) work on puzzles instead of watching TV. _____ frequently

3. I have (success, successfully) completed many kinds of puzzles. _____ successfully

4. I do not buy (any, no) puzzles that have fewer than a thousand pieces. _____ any

5. Three-dimensional puzzles are (good, well) puzzles to put together. _____ good

6. Some puzzles (continue, continually) repeat the same picture over and over. _____ continually

7. They are (especial, especially) hard to put together. _____ especially

8. My brother and I work (good, well) together on puzzles. _____ well

9. He doesn't have time to work on them (anymore, no more). _____ anymore

10. I feel great when I (final, finally) complete a puzzle. _____ finally

**At Home:** Write about something you like to do. Include at least three sentences that have adverbs.

McGraw-Hill Language Arts
Grade 4, Unit 6, Adverbs, pages 444–445

🔟

## Study Skills: Encyclopedia

- An **encyclopedia** is a reference work that contains articles on many subjects. It may be a single book, but it is more often a set of books or volumes.
- The volumes in a set of encyclopedias are labeled these two ways: numbers and alphabetically by subject.
- The last volume in an encyclopedia is the index, which lists all the subjects written about in the encyclopedia. The index is also arranged alphabetically by subject.

Complete each sentence with the number of the encyclopedia volume in which you would find an article.

1. An article on the horseshoe crab may be found in volume
9

2. To find out about coyotes, look in volume
4

3. Information on the Black Hills may be found in volume
2

4. Japanese literature may be looked up in volume
11

5. Radioactivity has an article in volume
16

6. You will find an article on Catherine the Great in volume
3

7. An article on Dodge City would be found in volume
5

8. Read the article about the country of Ethiopia in volume
6

9. Look up the painter Henri Matisse in volume
13

10. The article on the author of *Uncle Tom's Cabin*, Harriet Beecher Stowe, may be found in volume
18

**At Home:** Think of two subjects you would like to learn more about. In what volume of the encyclopedia shown on this page would you look for them?

**McGraw-Hill Language Arts**
Grade 4, Unit 6, Study Skills,
pages 452–453

10

---

## Vocabulary: Suffixes

- A **suffix** is a word part added to the end of a base word.

  work + er = worker   neat + ness = neatness
  slow + ly = slowly

- A suffix changes the meaning of the base word to which it is added.

| Suffix | Meaning |
|---|---|
| -er | person who |
| -ful | full of |
| -ion | an act or state of being. |
| -ly | like, full of in a certain way |
| -y | |
| -less | without |
| -ment | the result of |

Underline the word in each sentence that has a suffix. Write an equation for it. (See above for an example.)

1. It is very <u>windy</u> today.

wind + y = windy

2. I am showing my art project to my <u>teacher</u> today.

teach + er = teacher

3. Maybe if I walk <u>quickly</u>, my papers won't blow.

quick + ly = quickly

4. I was <u>successful</u> and made it to class on time.

success + ful = successful

5. My teacher gave me a <u>cheerful</u> greeting.

cheer + ful = cheerful

6. When she saw my art work, she expressed <u>amazement</u>.

amaze + ment = amazement

7. First her <u>expression</u> worried me.

express + ion = expression

8. "You used your materials in a <u>wonderful</u> way," she said.

wonder + ful = wonderful

9. The bright colors make it look so <u>joyful</u>.

joy + ful = joyful

10. My parents' <u>encouragement</u> helped me finish my art project.

encourage + ment = encouragement

10

**At Home:** Use a dictionary. Find and list words that are formed with the suffix -ist such as artist.

**McGraw-Hill Language Arts**
Grade 4, Unit 6, Vocabulary,
pages 454–455

Name _____ Date _____ **Reteach**

## Composition: Outlining

- When you need to organize ideas for a report, you can make an **outline**. Your writing topic is named in the outline **title**.
- The main topics are listed next to Roman numerals followed by periods. (I. II. III.)
- Each main idea will become a paragraph in your report.
- Subtopics are listed with capital letters followed by periods under each main topic. (A. B. C.) Subtopics are the details that support or explain a main topic in a paragraph.

Here is an outline that Julia prepared for a science report about sound.
Complete the outline by writing the correct numerals and letters on the lines.

**1.–10.**

Title: Sound

I. _____ A Kind of Energy

   A. _____ Sound waves caused by vibrations.

   B. _____ Waves travel at speed of sound.

II. _____ Characteristics of Sound

   A. _____ Volume

   B. _____ Pitch

III. _____ Unusual Sound Conditions

   A. _____ SONAR (sound navigation ranging)

   B. _____ Noise pollution

   C. _____ Hearing impairments

**At Home:** Think of a topic for a science report you would like to research. Outline your ideas. Use main topics, subtopics, and Roman numerals. Don't forget a title.

McGraw-Hill Language Arts
Grade 4, Unit 6, Composition Skills,
pages 456–457

10

**T49**